The Trials and Triumphs

Robert R. Fournier

Copyright © 2009 by Robert R. Fournier

The Trials and Triumphs
by Robert R. Fournier

Printed in the United States of America

ISBN 978-1-60791-475-4

All rights reserved solely by the author. The author guarantees all contents are original and do not infringe upon the legal rights of any other person or work. No part of this book may be reproduced in any form without the permission of the author. The views expressed in this book are not necessarily those of the publisher.

Unless otherwise indicated, Bible quotations are taken from The King James Version of the Bible. Copyright © 1972 by Thomas Nelson Inc.

www.xulonpress.com

Most of my book concerns my life, what happened to me as a child, what happened to me when I grew up, what my ambitions were and what I ended up doing and about the 51 years I spent on the Newark Police Department and some of the cases I worked on.

My name is Robert R. Fournier, and this is the story of my life. I was born on May 27, 1927 in Central Falls Rhode Island. My mother's name was Irene Nadeau Fournier, and my father's name was Joseph R. Fournier, commonly called Bob. My sister Cecile was one year older than me and born on April 19, 1926.

The earliest I can remember was when I was around four or five years old. My father was a drunk, always came home drunk and I can remember this as though it was happening now. One night that my father came home drunk, he was chasing my mother around hollering. My sister and I were screaming too, afraid that he was going to hurt her. My Grandfather, who lived downstairs, came up and said, "What is going on here?" and my father stopped because my grandfather was a big man and my father was on 5 feet 7 inches tall, so that was the end of that.

Well it got so bad that my mother divorced my father and had to go to work in Providence, Rhode Island. So she put both my sister and I into a boarding home. The ladies name was Aunt May and her husband Uncle Jim, these were not relatives of ours, my mother paid them to take care of us. Aunt May was a very mean woman. She didn't care about us she was just after the money, but Uncle Jim was a very nice man. I remember one day we were outside playing, before we went out she said, "Do not go in the garage." I wanted to get a comic book out of the garage, so I went into the garage to get it, she saw me and she hollered, "Bob, get up here!" They lived on the third floor, so I went upstairs, she told me to get in the bedroom, she had a whip in her hand, commonly called cat a nine tails, and it was a whip with nine leather straps. I was not going to stand for that, so I ran around the room, she was chasing me and whipping me, so I crawled under the bed, and she continued to whip me there. I was screaming, my sister came running in, so Aunt May started to whip her, soon enough Uncle Jim came in the room and she started to whip him too. He was finally able to get it away from her, and she sent us both to bed with no supper. She left to go visit the neighbor, and Uncle Jim made us supper with dessert and told us to clean up the dishes and put them away and to not tell her he fed us, and then sent us to bed. She was a very mean woman. Our mother came to visit us about two times a week, we begged her to get us out of there, we stayed with Aunt May and Uncle Jim for about a year.

Now onto my close relatives on my mother's side, My Grandfather was Joseph D. Nadeau and my Grandmother was Eva Maynard Nadeau. I did not know my Grandmother, as she passed away before I was born; they were both in Canada and were French Canadians. My Grandfather was a very nice man, he loved my sister and I very much. He used to tell me about some of the things that he did as a young man. In his twenties he went to California to visit his brother, and while he was there he decided to go to the Gold Rush in Alaska. Having no luck there, he returned to California, and learned how to do wallpapering. He eventually decided to go back to Pawtucket, Rhode Island and got into real estate and the insurance business. He was in this business for a very long time and became very wealthy. They had two daughters, my mother, Irene L. Nadeau and her sister

Cecile Nadeau. My mother told me about her mother, she said that she was very strict. One story she told me was that on Saturdays, both girls had to get on a ladder and clean the chandeliers throughout the house, piece by piece. They both loved their mom very much. My mother married my father, and Aunt Cecile married a man by the name of George King. My mother had my sister and me, and my aunt had my cousin Richard.

On my father's side, we had my grandmother and grandfather Fournier, who were also French. They had my Aunt Laura, Uncle Oscar, and Aunt Alice on my father's side. I did not know my Grandfather Fournier, as he had passed before I was born. I was told that he as a heavy drinker, and he was a Haberdasher, he sold men's clothes. My Grandmother used to hold me in her arms, in a rocker and would sing to me. I was five years old when she passed away. My mother took me to my Grandmother's house, there was a casket there, and when I approached the casket, I cried very loud and would not stop crying. I can still see that to this day. I loved her very much.

My uncle Oscar was not married. He drove a bakery truck, delivering baked goods to homes. He was a very heavy set man, and jolly. And he liked the woman, and they liked him too. Aunt Alice married Leo Callahan, and they had three children, Leo Jr., Barbara, and Lorraine. Aunt Glen married Lloyd Lawton, and they had two sons, Tommy and Charlie. As a young child I would visit them all the time. I loved all my aunts and uncles and cousins, as they all felt the same about me. All of my Aunts and Uncles are passed away; I do not know about my cousins, I lost contact with them when we moved away.

My mother met and married George Frost. I am not sure, but I think she married him to get us out of that house. He was a chauffeur, for rich people by the name of Deshler. They

The Trials and Triumphs

owned a mansion in Sagaponack, New York. My stepfather had a friend named Alex James; he was a Gardner for the Deshler home. We ended up moving in with him when I was about seven years old. Alex was a nice person and treated my sister and I well. We went to a two room schoolhouse, one room for first, second and third graders, the other room for fourth, fifth, and sixth graders. It was about six blocks from Alex's home and we walked to school. Let me tell you about George Frost.

My mother went from bad to worse on husbands. George was a heavy drinker and carouser. He did not care for me very much, but did like my sister. Most of the money he made was spent on drinking, and because of this we had to move to Bridgehampton, which was about seven miles from Sagaponek. We moved into a small two bedroom house and went to Bridgehampton High School, which housed graded one through twelve. We walked to school; it was about fourteen to fifteen blocks from where we lived. I was in the third grade, and one day I was sitting at my desk, which was near a window and I saw trees and poles falling down outside. I raised my hand and told the teacher what was happening, he ran to the window and saw we were having a hurricane. Soon enough we were rushed in the gym, and stayed there for about two hours until the wind subsided, and then we went home.

I had never seen so much devastation, trees, poles and power lines down. There were trees on houses. We luckily made it home okay, but only to find that a tree had fallen onto the kitchen of our home, which my mom had just left the kitchen right before the tree came down. My stepfather had eventually got a job at the Gas Company, meaning we moved again. We moved to a larger home about two blocks from the house we were living in. The house was owned by Charles Rogers; he was deaf and could not speak plainly. He was very nice to us and we called him Wargie. At this house, we each had a nice bedroom to ourselves. My stepfather was drinking away all of his money, so my mother got a job in a restaurant, washing dishes; all night long. She also cleaned the houses of rich people, so we could have food and clothes. Finally she got a job in a grocery store. She was a very hard worker, just so she could provide for my sister and me.

My stepfather was very mean to me when he was drinking, which was all the time. I was treated to physical and mental abuse all the time. He seemed to be an okay person if he was not drinking.

Our family was Catholic, and we went to a Catholic church that was about two blocks from the house. When I was about eight years old, I was in school and a priest from our church came to my school and asked if any catholic boys were interested in becoming Alter Boys. He had told us if we wanted too, we could come to the parsonage after school and he would teach us how to become altar boys. That afternoon, four of us went to the parsonage and the priest began teaching us Latin. Latin was used at that time during Mass. The first thing I remember learning was Adeum Que Latificote Uven Tudem Meum. For the next six weeks we went to the Parsonage to learn Latin, and when we finished that, he began to teach us how to serve in the mass. Following that he took each of us boys, one at a time to do this, we all ended up passing and became Alter Boys. I was picked as Leading Altar Boy and served Mass every Sunday. I ended up being an altar boy in different churches in the areas which we lived. I was an Altar Boy until I was seventeen years old.

One day I felt too ill to go to school, my parents were working and my sister went to school. I saw a truck pull into the driveway, and the driver knocked on the door; asking for Robert Fournier. He said he had a package for me and took a large crate out of his truck. I asked him to please put it in the garage and signed the paper, he left. I went out to the garage and started unpacking the crate and I found a beautiful red bike. The bike had fenders, lights, a horn, and balloon tires. I could not wait to ride it, and when my parents got home I took the bike for a ride downtown. Halfway downtown, there was a large tree with a sidewalk on both sides, I saw a girl coming toward me on a bike, so I went around the other side of the tree. Thinking she would go around the other side, much to my surprise she was on the same side and we crashed into each other. It put a big dent on my fender and bent the front tire. The bike as still drivable, and I kept it for a long time.

When I had opened that crate, there was a note in it from my father in Rhode Island. He stated, "I hope you like this bike and enjoy it." I thought that was very nice of him to do for me.

One night at about one in the morning, a car pulled into the driveway and dumped my stepfather out on the ground. He had been drinking all night, and my bedroom window faced the driveway, so I saw him. He was lying on the ground, yelling for help. My mother told us to let the s.o.b stay there, while he continued to yell. I thought that something was wrong, so I went outside and he was yelling that his leg was broken, while rolling back and forth. I dragged him to the house and got him inside and called for my mother. She came downstairs and checked his leg, which sure enough was broken. We called the doctor; he came to set his leg and told us to get him to the hospital, which was about six miles away. She took him and he was admitted to the hospital for about a week. As a result of this he had a bad limp for the rest of his life.

I always had chores to do, like mowing the grass. Wargie had a very big yard and it took a long time to mow it. I also had to take out the trash, bring in wood for the stove, wash and dry dishes, and help clean the house. One Sunday, my stepfather told me to mow the grass, and I did not feel like it, and decided to put it off because there was a movie called Jesse James, that I wanted to see very badly. My stepfather ended up taking my mother and sister to see it and I was left at home to mow the grass. When I grew up and was on my own, I went and saw that movie four different times.

My stepfather lost his job at the gas company because of his drinking. Wargie ended up passing away and his sister told us to move out, she was selling the house. My stepfather had a brother who lived on a farm outside of Granville, Ohio, so we borrowed a truck and loaded all our furniture and clothes in it. We left Bridgehampton and drove to Granville in the very cold winter. My sister and I had to ride in the back of the truck, with no heat and freezing. We took turns riding up front. His brother Jack owned a farm machinery place in Utica, Ohio and he took us in. We stayed there for awhile and then moved to Buckeye Lake, Ohio. We lived on 1st street about a hundred yards from the entrance to an Amusement Park, Buckeye Lake Park. It was the biggest amusement park in Ohio and I was about eleven years old.

We lived in a small two bedroom house with no running water and an outside toilet. My parents had a bedroom, and my sister had a bedroom; I lived on the front porch with a pull out couch, that I used for a bed. As in Rhode Island, I also had chores to do here. They included, carrying water, bringing in wood, mowing grass, shovel snow, and wash and dry dishes. I had to carry two pails to a pump about six blocks away, fill them with water and carry them home. Being a skinny kid this was quite a chore, and I had to do it every day. We had a big barrel outside that caught rain water for baths.

We lived across from Lake Lumber Company. They had a very large parking lot and cars would park there for free

The Trials and Triumphs

and go to the amusement park. At eleven years old, I came up with the idea to charge the cars to park there. I went to see the manager, Mr. Pryor, and asked him if I could charge people to park in the lot, on the condition I would give him half of what I made, he told me to go right ahead.

I made a sign that said "Parking 25 cents", and stood at the corner of 1st Street and Route 79, which was about thirty feet from the park entrance. People would stop and ask me where the parking was; I would jump on their running boards of their cars and take them to the lot. The park was open from 9 am to midnight, seven days a week. One the Fourth of July, I was very busy parking cars, the lot got full so I got permission to park them in our yard and the neighbor's yard. I ended up making a hundred dollars that day and the next day went to Mr. Pryor and gave him his share. He was surprised that I could make that much.

I had a lot of friends, to name a few; Russ Yontz, he was my best friend and Dick Walters, his father was the Fire Chief. He had a large lot next to the fire house, with a basketball bank board that we played at a lot. I went to Hebron High School, and we rode the bus to get to school. I got onto the Junior High School basketball team and loved to play. I also played football in high school.

At the age of twelve, I went to work in the park, this was my first job. I worked at the Pier Ballroom, where dance bands played. I was the ticket taker, and people would buy tickets for ten cents and dance on the huge dance hall. There were about six or seven entrances to the dance floor, and after the songs were over the ticket takers would herd the people off the floor for the next dance. I worked there for that summer and the next year I worked at the Crystal Ballroom, doing the same thing. My sister worked at the swimming pool, which was directly below the ballroom. My mother also sold tickets that were in front of the rides and my stepfather did odd jobs in the park. All the name band played in the park, and I got to see most of them. Harry James, Benny Goodman, Tommy Dorsey, Jimmy Dorsey, Glen Miller, and Bunny Berrigan, just to name a few.

Bunny Berrigan was a great guy, he led the band and he played the trumpet and could he play that trumpet. There was a ball diamond at the back of the parking lot and Bunny and some of his band members would come down and play softball with us kids. One day I was at bat, Bunny was pitching, and all of a sudden, here comes my mom. She grabbed me by the ear and said you get home and do your chores and led me away by my ear. I was so embarrassed and Bunny was laughing at me. The next day he came to me in the park and said don't feel bad about me laughing at you, I know how it is. He was a great guy.

The next year when the park opened, I worked in the shooting gallery and the year after that I worked several rides. When I was about sixteen years old, my stepfather went into the excavating business. He had several bulldozers and a crane and he had people who worked for him. At that time they were building the Kaiser Aluminum Plant, and he had his equipment working there for him. He got me a job at the carpenter shop, I was the errand boy. I ran errands all over the plant and was making 72 and a half cent per hour. I had a real high voice when I was that age, so the guys at the shop started calling me Alice. They were just having fun with me and I understood that so it did not bother me. I was still getting abuse from my stepdad at this time, both physically and verbally and he would cuss at me. He made me feel like I was useless. One day I had enough, my mother and he had left and my sister was visiting a friend, I packed a bag and had save one hundred dollars. I left a note to my mother and told her I had enough and I was leaving.

I walked the back way from Buckeye Lake to Hebron, thumbed a ride to Newark and went to the Penn Railroad

Station. I caught a train to New York City and went to the New Haven Railroad; from there I got a train ride to Providence, Rhode Island. I called my Grandfather in Pawtucket and asked if he would pick me up, he did. He took me to his house and I told him about all the abuse from my stepdad and that I had ran away. The next day he took me to Aunt Laura's house and I asked if I could stay there with her and Uncle Jack. After explaining the situation I was in, they both agreed to let me stay. My father lived there too at that time, and was working at a gas station.

My cousin Jackie also lived there, and she and a girlfriend worked at a factory making guns. It was 1943, and World War Two was underway. I decided to apply at a job at the factory and got the job. My job was pulling guns off a skid and taking them to be oiled. During break time I had gotten friendly with this guy and he showed me how to put the guns together. Eventually an opening came up in the reassembly section and I got the position. I was finally making good money.

I had walked away from school, and I should have never done that. My mother and stepfather found out where I was and came back and got me. Since I was only sixteen, I had to go back with them to Ohio. I went back to school and got out of the tenth grade. I wanted my mother to sign for me to go into the Navy, but she wouldn't. When I was seventeen, I asked her again and she did.

June 6, 1944, D-Day. This was the day I went into the Navy. I reported to Columbus, Ohio and was put on a train and taken to Great Lakes Training Center in Illinois for boot camp. I was in boot camp for about seven weeks and then got a ten day leave. I came home for my leave and after it was over I reported back to Columbus. I was then put on a troop train and taken to Shoemaker, California Naval Base for assignment. I was there for about two weeks and then put on a transport ship in San Francisco, and was put out to sea. We had no idea where we were going, and there were about 200 of us, all new sailors. We ended up in Milne Bay, New Guinea. In the middle of the war with the Japanese. The Japanese were up in the hills; this is where they ran after the marines had chased them. We were there for about four weeks, 50 of us were then put on a small ship and taken to Finch haven, New Guinea to a P.T. boat base.

We reported to the Commander of the base, he asked us what type of assignment we would like and I wanted to be a store keeper. All the store keeper assignments had been filled so I was made a ships cook. I worked in the galley for the troops. There were five or six cooks there and eventually I was able to become a store keeper. I was put in charge if all the foods that were needed for the base. I was called Jack of the Dust; still I have no idea why they chose this name. When food supplies got low I would order more. The navy moved fast, I had enlisted in June, and in September I was in the middle of the war in New Guinea.

In the latter part of September, we were told we were going to invade Leyte Gulf in the Philippines, and that we were going to set up a P.T. boat base there. After the invasion all of our equipment was loaded onto a large transporter ship, we started for the Philippines and that was in early October of 1944. On the way it was very foggy and one night it was very hot. Several of us went topside to sleep, I could hear the fog horns wailing. I sat up and saw the bow of a cargo ship headed right for the middle of our ship. I yelled and told everyone to look. Just then both ships started turning away, but it was too late. The cargo ship hit us, in the fantail; which is the backend of our ship, and put a gigantic hole in it. We were taking in water, so they shut up the compartment where the water was coming in and we limped back to Hollandia, New Guinea. We missed out on the invasion of Leyte. It took several weeks to transfer all the equipment to a new ship, but then orders had been made that we were going to set up the boat base in Mindoro Island. This was in the Philippines, which was north of Leyte. The marines had invaded Mindoro, and had chased the Japanese into the hills. We landed on the beach at Mindoro Island and set up the base. We pitched tents on the beach, and that is where we stayed until everything was secured. We were there until the war was declared over. I believe it was around August of 1945.

When we landed on Mindoro Island, we found that the Navy Seabees had already landed several months before us. They had set up a large camp; the kitchen was in a medium sized tent and a large tent behind it for the mess hall. There were about six small stoves, what we could call camping stove and a medium sized refrigerator and tables to work on. We used large pots for cooking, and the mess hall had picnic tables with benches for the crews. I started working in the kitchen from 4 am to 12 noon and we had our tents pitched about 400 yards away. At 3:30 am I had to walk to the kitchen in the dark and it was kind of scary as the Japanese were still in the hills around us. The P.T. boat docks were about another 300 yards away from the kitchen.

There was a Navy base about five or six miles away from our base with a large air strip and sometimes the Japanese would come over to bomb the Navy Base and the air strip. The twin 50 guns would go off, that meant to head for a bomb shelter, which we did. We had a large trench close to our tent and close to the kitchen and our base never did get hit. We had many large palm trees around our base and they kept us kind of hidden. I worked in the kitchen for about six months.

The Seabees were still there, making our base larger. They built a much larger kitchen and a large mess hall, and they also built us large tents with wood floors and round tables in the middle which slept five men. We had about 80 men in

The Trials and Triumphs

our division, about nine or ten were ship cooks. They built a large warehouse to keep the food stuff and they needed a person to take care of this area. Since I had experience doing this, the Commander of our unit asked me if I would do this job. I thought about it and agreed. I became Jack of the Dust again, and had to take inventory and make an order for the food that we needed and turn it into the commander.

Things were beginning to be secure on our base. I had become 3rd Class Petty Officer and around August of 1945 and there was a USO Show at the Navy Base. The name of the show was Oklahoma and six or seven of us drove to the Navy Base to see it. At intermission the Captain of the Navy Base came to the stage and announced the Japanese Government had accepted the terms of the surrender. The war was over in August 1945. I figured I was going to be stuck overseas for another year; a directive came out the said if you shipped over for two years you could go home for 30 days and get $200 mustering out pay. Six of us signed up for that, and in September we packed up all of our gear and we were put on a L.S.T and headed for Manila, in the Philippines. We had all of our records with us and everything pertaining to us was in our folders that we carried. An old sailor on the LST told us we would be sending to the Cavite Naval Station and we would have to wait 30 to 60 days before we could get a ship back to the states. He told us since we had all of our records with us we need to go to port authority in Manila and catch our own ship home.

We arrived in Manila and went to the Lagarda Hotel, on Lagarda Street. We got several rooms and it was evening time so we decided to go to a large restaurant downstairs. There were a lot of people there and at the table next to us there were some WAC's (women's army corps) and soldiers. We told them we were going back to the states and they were going back too, the next day. The SS Lurline, a Matson Liner, so jokingly we said we would probably see them on board.

The Trials and Triumphs

We had one guy that could talk himself into anything, while the rest of us were asleep he and another guy went to Port Authority and found where the SS Lurline was docked and went to the Captain of the ship and asked if we could go back with them. If we worked our way back, the Captain agreed. About 8 am the next morning, they came back to the hotel and told us they found a ship and we packed our belongings and headed to the docks. They did not tell us it was the SS Lurline and when we got there we were taken to the Captains office and they told us that we would run the chow lines every morning and evening. He had one of his men take us to a stateroom, and I could not believe what I saw. It was plush, had 3 bunk beds with springs and mattresses, carpet on the floor, private bathrooms and comfortable chairs. We had not seen springs and mattresses for almost a year. When we got settled in, we all got topside and saw a lot of the WAC's lined up on the dock. There were also some soldiers started to come aboard. The ship had 600 WAC's, 200 soldiers, and 6 sailors. We had a lot of fun on the way back; it took us six days to get back to San Francisco. When we got back we went out on the town, we went to a tattoo parlor and each got a tattoo on our arm. The next day we reported to Shoemaker Navy Base, which was across the bridge from San Francisco. We turned in our records and got a physical, and received our 30 day leave papers and $200. We were all to report back to Shoemaker when our leaves were up.

    I took a train to Columbus, Ohio and caught a bus to Newark. I called my mother and she came and got me and took me to Buckeye Lake, and I spent my leave having fun with my friends. The park was still open and I saw all the people I use to work with and the welcomed me home. My cousin Richard came to the lake to spend some time me. We were practically like brothers and spent a lot of time together. My leave was about over and I caught a train back to Shoemaker California Navy Base and reported in, I had to wait to be drafted on a ship.

We were told we would probably have to wait six to eight weeks before we were assigned to a ship. I met this other sailor and we went out on a pass. I did not know where to go and he had been there longer than me. He told me there was a school that had dances ever Friday evening from 6pm to 11pm. So we went to the school and there were a lot of people there. I used to like to dance so I looked around for a girl, and I saw a prey blonde with blue eyes, so I asked her to dance. We introduced ourselves and her name was Gerry Wright. She was 17 years old and was very nice and kind of shy. We talked awhile and danced, she was a senior in high school. She came with her mother and after the dance she took me to meet her mother. I asked if she came every Friday, and she said yes. We had quite a few dances before we left and I asked her if she would dance with me again if I came back and she agreed. I felt like she liked me. After several Friday nights her mother invited me to her house. I had the feeling that her mother liked me too. The following Monday, I went to their house and met her 3 brothers who were older then her. I had a good time with the whole family and asked her to go to the movies with me and with the approval of her mother, she said yes. We became quite attached and every time I would get a pass out I would go to her house. We could go to a movie, take a walk or go to dances.

Eventually I fell in love with her. And she told me she loved me too. I never felt like that before for any girl. About that time I got assigned to a ship, the USS Benevolence, a hospital ship. I was assigned to work in the galley. We were leaving in a week, out to see and I said my goodbyes to Gerry and her family. I asked if she would write to me and she said she would. We headed out to sea and were told we were going to Bikini Islands, for the two Atom Bomb test that was about to happen.

We arrived at Bikini Atoll, went ashore and had a few beers. We went back to the ship and pulled out about 15 miles because the next day the bomb test would start. It was the next day that they Atom Bomb exploded, we had to turn our back away and cover our eyes. After the explosion, as far as we were from the blast you could see the large mushroom cloud rising into the air. It was kind of scary. One day after we got back to the Atoll, we went ashore again, it had done a lot of damage. We then pulled back again form the Atoll and one week later the next explosion happened. They had pulled a lot of old ships in the Atoll, we were about 7 miles away. When the explosion happened, it lit up the whole area. We could see all the old ships, it was so bright and the mushroom cloud began to rise. We pulled back into the Atoll and some of the ships were sunk, some were listing. We anchored about 400 yards from a large Japanese ship and the next morning the Japanese ship had sunk. We were not allowed to go on land, but it was quite a site. They checked our ship and found a slight amount of radio activity in our bilges. We were ordered to go back to the states and when we pulled into San Francisco Bay and anchored we got a one day pass and then had to report back to the ship the next day. They had found very little radio activity in our ship, so out to sea again and we were ordered to China this time.

We headed out to sea in the Pacific Ocean; it took us 10 to 12 days to get to the Yellow Sea off of Tsingtao, China. We docked on Pier 1 and were docked there for eight months. We were allowed liberty every night, so several of us went to town. A troop truck would take us from the dock into the city of Tsingtao. Being sailors we went to a night club, it was always the same club and had a nice dance hall. We would get a table and the Chinese girls would come around,

The Trials and Triumphs

this pretty girl named Soufan always came to our table, she would sit with us and got stuck one of my friends. We went there about every night, and my friend and I had our picture taken with Soufan. I carried that picture for a long time, she was such a nice person, but somewhere along the way I lost her picture. I probably had it for about 25 years. One day four of us decided we wanted to go horseback riding, so we found a stable and rented four horses. They were so small, like ponies, the man that rented the horses to us told us to not go on any hills with them, because the Nationalist Chinese were fighting the communists. But we were crazy young sailors, so to the hills we went. When we got there we could hear shooting and several bullets hit the rocks above us. You should have seen us get out of there, and we never did that again.

    I was assigned to the galley again. One day I was putting meat in the oven and I had a cigarette in my mouth, the Lt. Commander saw me and chewed me out royally. He told me that if he caught me doing that again, he would put me on report. I never did it again, and he did not like me after that. I worked in the galley for about two months, and was assigned the name of Jack of the Dust again. The galley had a small storeroom, with a desk and chair. When the ships cooks needed anything they would come and get it from me. The galley was right across from my office, I would take inventory and when more food was needed I would order it. We had a larger food storeroom in another part of the ship and I was also responsible for that too. A memorandum came down from the Captain, they were starting a ship basketball team and if anyone wanted to get on the tem you could sign up. I loved playing basketball, so I signed up. I made the team and there were only two other ships tied up at a different dock and about five other ships anchored by the bay. We were to play all of the teams from the other ships plus teams from two Marine bases. We played and practiced

The Trials and Triumphs

at a large school in the middle of Tsingtao. We had a very good team, about 10 of us from our ship. We had a tournament after three months and won the championship. We were given a nice trophy and were the champions of Tsingtao. Our Captain was very proud of us.

Gerry and I wrote to each other quite frequently. I found a store with beautiful pajamas with sequins on them, they were all different colors. I sent those to Gerry. We left China on the Yellow Sea and headed back to the states. There was a very bad storm and our ship got into a trough, with waves higher than the ship on both sides. The quartermaster steering the ship had a very hard time getting us out of that trough. We finally got turned and headed out of the Yellow Sea; I thought we were going to sink. I sure was scared. We got back to San Francisco, and docked in a shipyard for repairs.

The first liberty I got was to go see Gerry. She was very aloof, and did not say much. I asked what was wrong, and she said nothing. I figured she was seeing someone else. I said goodbye and left, that was the last time that I saw her. I went back to the ship and decided I would make the Navy my career. I wanted to be promoted to 2nd Class Petty Officer. I asked if I could take the test, he said no. I knew that he did not like me so I said okay and my enlistment was about up. I left the Navy, and went back home. My parents had moved to Newark, Ohio, so I moved in with them. I did not know what I was going to do, my mother had found an article in the newspaper, and it said you could apply to go to Hotel Training School in Washington, D.C. under the G.I. Bill, at no cost.

I applied and got accepted. Everything was paid for, tuition, room and board, and food. I arrived in D.C. and went to the rooming house and roomed with another guy that was going to the school too. He showed me around, we caught a bus and went to the school and registered. I was learning how to be a hotel manager. It was an 18 week school, and it was interesting, I enjoyed it. Two weeks before graduation, I was called to the office and was told there was an opening for a chef at the Commissioned Officers Mess, in Quantico, Virginia, a Marine base. They wanted to know if I would be interested, it was a long cry from being a hotel manager, but I said I would check it out. I caught a bus to the base and went to the office of the Mess Hall. I met with the head chef, and he asked me a few questions, and said if I wanted the job, I could have it. It was like a hotel with rooms upstairs that would be mine. I went back to D.C., packed my stuff, went to the school and advised them I took the job and was told that I would graduate in two weeks. They said I would have to be at the ceremony to get my diploma, which I did. I became 2nd Chef and enjoyed that job; I worked from 6am to 6pm and eventually became 1st chef. Once or twice a week I would go to D.C. to a night club and that is where I met Cindy Lou Ray, from Columbus, Mississippi. She was very cute, dark hair, and blue eyes. We danced a lot and she took me to her house, where I met her aunt, whom she lived with. Every chance I had, I would go to see her.

The head chef had a 1941 Chevrolet that he wanted to sell. It was a good looking car and he wanted $100 for it. I bought it, but I did not have a driver's license, so I took a driving test in the town of Quantico, passed and got my license. I had a car to go see Cindy instead of riding the bus. We would take rides all over D.C. I had taken her to the Marine base and showed her around, there was a tennis court, golf course and just all kinds of attractions, and we had a great time. The next time I had asked her to come to the base, I picked her up and when I drove to D.C. to get her, she got real mad and said she and her aunt were moving. She told me not to bother her anymore and I left and never saw her again, another romance gone badly (the story of my life).

I had received a phone call from my mother saying that my stepfather had beaten her real bad, drunk again. I was ready to do him bodily harm. I asked for some time off so I could go to Ohio to help my mother. She had always done her best to help my sister and me. I got home and saw her condition, bruises and welts. I got very angry and confronted him, and he said he was very sorry and that he had been very drunk and it would never happen again. I felt sorry for him, because I believed he was sorry, and it never did happen again. To be sure, I called the head chef and told him that I had to quit my job to stay home with my mother. I explained to him what happened and he agreed I should stay with her. So I was out of a job again.

I got a job working at the L&K Restaurant at 4th and Locust. I worked 11pm to 7am, it was opened all night and I worked as a grill cook, making $35 a week. I became very lonely and wanted female companionship, the woman who lived across the alley from us was my mother's good friend, and we would visit her. I told her my problem and she said she knew a nice girl; she would call her and have her come over so I could meet her. I was 21 years old at the time. Her name was Margaret Eleanor Porterfield, we were introduced to each other and she seemed like a real nice girl, she was 20 years old. We went out to the movies and to dinners. She lived with her mother and father on Wildwood Avenue we went for rides in my 1941 Chevy and became much attached. We liked each other really well. She worked at Doneffs Bakery downtown and made $20 a week. Her mother was very strict and made her work around the house a lot. Her foster parents were Raymond and Pat Porterfield; they had adopted her from the Children's Home when she was 10 years old. She liked to be called Eleanor.

Eleanor and I got along real good, and liked each other very much. I asked her to marry me around Christmas time 1948 and we set the date for August 1, 1949. On that date we got married at St. Francis Church, we were both Catholic and had been going to church every Sunday. Her parents were Catholic too, and I think that is why they liked me. It was a small wedding, just friends and family. It was not formal, we both wore suits. After the wedding we had a reception at the Hull Place, and left the reception and headed for New Jersey. We went to visit my Aunt Ceil, Uncle Stan and Cousin Richard; he was going to college close to where they lived. It was not far from New York City, so my cousin took us there. He knew the city like the back of his hand. We were all over the city, Empire State Building, Time Square, Grand Central Station, Central Park, Empire State Building, Statue of Liberty, Large Store and finally Coney Island. It was quite a day; we went back to Aunt Ceils house. The next day we took a ferry to Bear Mountain and stayed there all day. And two day later we headed back home. We had a one bedroom apartment on North 5th street in Newark and in November 1948 she became pregnant. Around September 1949, I was still working at the restaurant and several Newark Police Department Detectives came in for breakfast every morning. I would talk to them and told them I was not satisfied with my job and salary. Henry Hall, one of the detectives told me that I should go and sign up for the test at the Civil Service Commission because there were four vacancies on the Police Department. I told him that I would do that. At the time you had to be 5'8 inches tall and weigh no less than 155 pounds. I was six foot tall but only 150 pounds, so I started to eat more and drinking milkshakes. Anything I could to gain weight. I went to the Civil Service Commission to sign up for the test. It was at Newark High School. They sent me to Doctor Busman for a physical. When I went for it I only weighed 154.5 pounds, and I asked him to please put down

The Trials and Triumphs

155, and he did. I took the test in October 1949, and was told they would let us know if we passed. I told my boss that I had taken the test for the Police Department and he fired me on the spot. I had no job, a pregnant wife and I could not pay my rent. We moved in with my Mother and drunken stepfather. I needed a job; my stepfather was in the excavating business. He said I will get you a job and he did. They were building a dynamite factory way out on Dry Creek Road. My job was digging footers and ditches with a pick and shovel. I did that about two weeks and did not care for it at all. In the middle of October 1949, my stepfather came to the site and said he had a letter for me, I opened it and it was from the Civil Service Commission. I had passed the test for the Police Dept. I was to report to the department on November 10, 1949 to be sworn in as a Police Officer.

    The appointment letter said that I should report to the Newark Police Department at 9am in uniform to be sworn in. I went to the department and talked to Bernard Howarth, who was working the desk, I asked him what I needed in the way of a uniform. I needed breeches, putts, a dark blue uniform shirt, black tie, Sam brown belt, holster, handcuff case, handcuffs, 5 point hat, black shoes, and dark blue coat. I asked where I could get these things and he told me I can buy them from retired officers. I was told to see Bob Cass, who was starting the department on November 7th. He would tell me who to go talk to about getting these items. I was also told I had to buy my own revolver.

    Cass worked at a body shop on West Main Street, behind the Salvation Army. I went there and met him for the first time. He was to become my best friend during the time on the department. He told me who to see about buying parts for the uniform and told me to see Sgt. Denny Harris, who worked the desk from 12 midnight to 8am; he had a gun for sale. I found all the parts I needed for the uniform and also got Denny Harris to sell me a 38 Smith and Wesson revolver with a 6 inch barrel and white grips.

November 10, 1949 at 9am, I was sworn in as a Newark Police Officer by safety director Frank Robinson. Chief of Police Gail Christman game me my badges, a rule book and a call box key and told me to report to the station at 4om to go out with Ptl. Arthur Nutter Sr. The Police department was made up like this: 1 Chief, 1 Chief of Detectives, 1 Captain, 3 Sergeants, and 34 Patrolmen. We had 4 cruisers, 2 marked cars, 2 plain cars. The 2 marked cars were 2 man cruisers, 1 plain car for the 2 patrolmen assigned as Detectives and 1 plain car assigned to the Chief of Police. There were 5 walking districts, they were called Beats. I marked car with 2 uniformed officers were assigned to the North and East section of the city and the other marked car with 2 uniformed officers were assigned to the South and West section of the city. That was our department.

At 3:45pm I went to the department and met Arthur Nutter Sr. He had been on the department for over 25 years and had been walking the beat on the North side of the square for 18 years. It was the best thing to happen to me, having him break me in. He was a very good police officer and everyone on the beat respected him. As we walked around the beat we talked and he showed me what a beat officer did, check the area and business places, go down alleys and check the doors at the rear of the business places. We would go in the bars to keep order and everyone on that beat really loved Pappy Nutter, he was called Pappy by the other officers on the force because he had been on the force for so long.

I had to sell my Chevy, so my next problem was how I was going to get to work at the Police Department. Bob Cass had told me that they City Rapid Transit Buses would take uniformed officers, such as police, fire and postmen, on the bus for free. I caught the bus at Hollander Street and Channel

Street and that is where I met Sergeant Lester Hall. Sgt. Hall was the desk Sgt. On the 4pm to 12 midnight shift, we then went to Maple Avenue where Bob Cass got on the bus. We then went downtown, got off the bus and walked down on alley to the department. The buses ran until midnight.

As I said before, Pappy Nutter showed me what I had to do while walking the North Side of the square. As he was showing me what to do, we were talking and he told me 4 things that will help me during my police career. First, always treat people decently, be friendly with the people you will meet, be kind and treat them like you would want to be treated and this applies to people you might even arrest. Second, never accept any money from anyone, because if you do, you will be beholding to them. Third, always play your hunches. And fourth, there will come a time that you will not know what to do, always use good common sense. I always used that advice during my career, and it always paid off. He showed me the call boxes and how to use them. There were five call boxes on the North side. You had to call into the station every hour, the North side calling in every hour on the hour, and the South side calling in every half hour. We walked the beat until 11:45pm called off on the call box at 4th and West Main Street and then went to the station. I thanked Pappy for showing me what to do.

The next night I went out on the South side beat with Roy Waldren from 4pm to 12 midnight. He showed me who the south side district and there were a lot of bars on that district. We had to go into bars to keep the trouble down, and would generally stay in the bars for 10 minutes, then go to another bar. We checked the district, shaking door knobs in and out of the alleys. There was an alley he took me in behind the Bargain Shoe Store, he said this is where Officer Beasley was shot and killed. It was very eerie, and I could not wait to get out of that alley. At 11:45pm we called off on the callbox and went into the station. I thanked Roy for showing me what to do on his district.

The next night I went in the North and East cruiser district with Bernard Howarth and Jon McDonnell. They showed me what they had to do, check the whole area of North and East city and answer calls. It was real cold and there was ice on the street. We got a call to East Main Street and Hazelwood, ref an accident. When we got there it was so slippery, that you could hardly stand up. They showed me how to take an accident report. For 4pm to 12 midnight shift it was very quiet. At the end of the night I thanked them for showing me what to do.

The next night I went in the South and West cruiser with Art Hartley and Paul Stotler. They showed me how to check that district. I don't remember the calls we got but it was very quiet and very cold. The North side beat officer was on vacation, so I was assigned to that beat. I had gone out with someone for 4 days and here I was walking the beat by myself. That is all the training I had received. I did not know beans from apple butter about being a police officer. But I muddled through it; I worked that beat for 2 weeks. It was very quiet on the North side, the bars closed at midnight there and there were no people on the street, no cars on the roads and so I checked the business places, and made my calls to the station every hour. The North side breath man had to come to the station around 6am to feed the prisoners and sweep the floors at the department. He would also empty the wastebaskets, and I was glad to do that, it got me out of the cold.

When the officer came back from vacation, the South side 12 midnight to 8am beat officer went on vacation and I was assigned to that beat. It was the same thing, no one out. I had to check the businesses n and out of the alleys and had to go into that alley that Officer Beasley was killed in, it was pitch black and I walked very slowly, shining my flashlight back and forth. Let me tell you, my heart was jumping and I was glad when I got out of that alley. I worked that job for 2 weeks and when he got back from vacation, I was assigned to work the South side walking district, called the short beat. It wasn't very short at all; it took 2 hours to cover the whole beat. I was working from 9pm to 5am. Back in the horse and buggy days, officers were walking beats on all edges of Newark, called long beats. So I was glad I got the short beat. I had bars on this district too that I had to go into. I have to tell you a story told to me by an older officer. Back in the horse and buggy when officers walked very long beats, the hired officers for more brawn then brains. This officer was walking his beat and came on to Tuscarawas Street, and he found a dead horse. Knowing that he had to leave a written report on the incident, he did not know how to spell Tuscarawas, so he dragged the horse to Cedar Street and said he found the horse there.

I worked the South short beat for about six months. Pappy Nutter got transferred to the Detective Division and his downtown north side beat 4pm to 12midnight came open and I was assigned to it. It was a welcome beast as 9pm to 5am shifts were not to my liking. This was May of 1950. There were many people downtown, and it was a nicer atmosphere. Every evening in front of the Newark Trust Company, many lawyers, judges and the Advocate editor would hang out and talk. I would stop when I was walking my beat, and talk with them. I met them all and I could tell that they liked me, they were friendly and over the years I would meet them in court as a witness. I am so glad I met them, as they would take it easy on me when I was testifying from the stand. You know how lawyers can get when they are cross examining you. And the Newark Advocate Owner and editor, Frank Spencer, really liked me. Everything I did referring criminal activity, that I worked on or would solve, he would make sure my name was in the paper. That helped me to keep a scrapbook about some of the things I got involved with over the years.

The best part of the beat was that you got to make personal contact with people, which ended up helping me a lot during my police career. I had contact with cab drivers, hotel clerks, waitresses, customers in the bars, people that I met on the street, and even people would arrest for minor crimes. A lot of these people would be my sources of information when I became a detective. I really liked the beat that I was walking. On July 21, 1950, my first son was born, John Anthony Fournier. I was so proud. He was a lively child, and I loved him very much. We had a lot of fun together as he was growing up.

My mother found an article in the newspaper that veterans could apply to buy a house with $200 down, under the G.I. Bill of rights. I went to realtor Josephine Cain Wright, and she showed me a nice 2 bedroom house on North 28th Street. I put my money down, and had a nice house finally. My family moved in about October 1950. I still took the bus to work, and was still on the north side of the square beat. I worked that beat for about ten months, and could see why Pappy kept it for 18 years.

I bought a 1948 Cadillac, it was a good car, and every year we got a two week vacation, we would go to New Jersey or New York, sometimes Long Island. I got us in debt over my head, trying to improve our house and we had to sell it. We moved into and apartment on Cedar Street.

April 21, 1951, I was working the east side walking district on the 12 midnight shift to 8am. It was very cold for April, and very quiet. It was around 4:30am and I walked into the station, Roy Waldren was there and Clay Shepard was working the desk. He wanted to go eat so Roy took over the desk and we were talking. Around 5am the door opened and this guy and woman walked in, the man had blood all over his face and hands and said that he had a good one for us. I just killed a woman he says, the woman that was with him was his wife. His name was Jamison. I was waiting for Roy to start questioning him, but he wasn't saying anything. So I asked him his name and where did this happen? I brought him and his wife into the Chief's office and he said he went to his friend's house on Boylston Avenue and his friend was at work. So his wife let him in and he had been drinking heavily. The wife was very pretty and he made advances towards her, she resisted and he got mad, so he started beating her and knocking her to the floor. He pulled her nightgown up to her chest so he could molest her. She fought him and then he choked her to death. He left and went home to tell his wife what had happened so she brought him to the station. I sent a cruiser to the scene. The doors were locked and they looked in the windows and said they saw a woman lying on the floor. I told them to standby and called the acting Captain Wheeler who had gone home. The one Captain that we had worked from 8pm to 4am, and I told him what happened, he told me that he would be right back to the station. When he arrived at the station, Clay was back at the station from lunch, so I asked the Captain if I could go to the scene. He agreed and when we got there the two officers were on the front porch, unable to get in. I went around to the side of the house and found a screen porch; the door was locked so I pulled the screen out and crawled onto the porch and unlocked the door. The door to the kitchen was unlocked and we all went into the living room. The woman lying on the floor, a nightgown pulled up to her chest and blood all over her face and a bloody handprint on her stomach. She was dead, the Captain told me to go upstairs to check it out and I got to the top of the stairs, there was a bed with 2 little children in it. A little boy sat up and said hello, I said hello back and headed back down the steps. I got halfway down the steps and both children started to cry for their mother, let me tell you, it brought a lump to my throat. I felt so sorry for them, with their mother downstairs murdered. Jamison was convicted and sentenced to life in prison. That was my first big case, it made the newspaper and that is what started my scrapbook. After that every time my name was put in the paper, I cut it out and put it in my book.

July 1951, I was assigned to the 4pm to 12 midnight south and west cruiser with Bob Cass as my partner. We got involved in many situations. Here are a few.

One evening around 8pm we got a call of a child hit by a car on North 11th and Church Street. We were not very far away and got there in about 5 minutes. When we arrived, we found a little 5 year old girl lying on the street. She was still breathing, so I called for an ambulance. She had blood coming out of her eyes, nose, mouth and ears. She was a cute little girl. What happened was a man was at the red light on Church Street waiting to make a left turn onto 11th Street. There was a church at the corner and people were beginning to leave the church. The light turned green, and the young man turned slowly, according to witnesses, the little girl ran between two parked cars and was struck by the car. She was sent flying and landed about 20 feet away, where we found her. The ambulance picked her up and headed for the hospital. The girl died on the way. It was heart breaking to see that and I have never forgotten it. I can still see it to this day.

Another incident, a car came skidding from West Main Street onto South 5th Street, he was traveling very fast. We started to chase him down National Drive to Linville Road. We were going about 100 mph, Cass was driving and going around curves he had to be going faster than us cause he was pulling ahead of us by about 4 or 5 miles. We saw him turn left on a dirt road and we had gotten close as the chase started, so we were able to get his plate number. We came close to where he turned, but we were going so fast we slid right by the road and had to back up to make the turn. There were all kinds of dust from the dirt road, so we had to slow down. We went about 1 mile and found cows in the middle of the road. So that was the end of the chase. We located the farmer and helped him get the cows off the road. The next night we saw the guy in the car downtown, same plate number. We stopped him and asked him to come to the station, which he did. We took him into an office and asked him about the chase and we were joking with him about how he got away from us. He admitted that it was him and we gave him a ticket for reckless operation. He was 20 years old and today this young man is the Pastor of a church. And he has been for some time.

    We got a domestic call on Elmwood Avenue. When we got there the lady let us in, her husband was there, drunk and very nasty. She said I want him taken out of here, so we said lets go. He started for another room; she hollered he had a gun in there. We tackled him and got him down and handcuffed him. Took him to the department and locked him up. We charged him with domestic violence.

    Another call we got involved with was also on Elmwood Avenue. My stepfather had remarried, and he had come home drunk and beat her up. When I got there I was surprised to see who it was, she asked us to get him out of there. So we put him in my cruiser and headed for the department. I told Cass that who this man was, and told my ex stepfather that if we gave him a break, that he could not go back home until he was sober. Cass and I took him to the Arcade Hotel, watched him check in and again reminded him to not go home until he was sober, and if he did we would arrest him and put him in jail. I don't know why I did this; I think I felt sorry for him.

The Trials and Triumphs

Cass and I had a great working relationship. We enjoyed each other's company and what we were doing. We patrolled our districts, answered calls, took accident reports, stopped fights, and treated people decently. We were friendly with everyone that we met, even those we had to arrest.

One night we were coming down Where Avenue, headed for Union Street when I started laughing. About what, I don't know. I was laughing uncontrollably and Bob asked what I was laughing about, I said I didn't know. Then he started laughing too. We stopped at a red light, and by that time we were both laughing uncontrollably. We sat at that light through about ten different changes, continued to laugh and not know what we were laughing at. That was just some of the nutty things that happened to us.

My wife became pregnant again, our relationship was going badly. As I was never home, I was involved in a lot of things like playing basketball on the American Legion Basketball Team; Cass was on the team too. We were in the City League and had a very good team as we won the City League Championship. As a bunch of younger officers, about 10 or 12 of us wanted to get a Club House for the Fraternal Order of Police Association. This would be a place to meet, the City Hall was near the department and it had three floors, the third floor was never used. So we asked the Mayor if we could use one of the rooms there and he agreed. So all of us when we were off duty would go up there and fix it up. We wallpapered, sanded the floors, painted, and got 2 desks and a lot of chairs and we built a bar. It took us about 3 weeks to finish it; after we got it done we had our first meeting there. It turned out really nice. We elected officers and I was elected Master at Arms and doorkeeper. Over the years I was Treasurer, Secretary, Vice President, and President of the lodge. We had that room for a long time and a meeting ever month.

The Trials and Triumphs

Around December 1951, Cass and I were transferred to the 12 midnight to 8am North and East cruiser. One night we got a call on Market Street referred to as a domestic. When we got there we went up on the porch and knocked on the door. A lady hollered from upstairs that her husband beat her up and she wanted him locked up. We asked where he was and she told us out somewhere. Just then someone said what do you guys want? There was a man standing on the ground, and we told him that his wife said that he beat her up and wanted him locked up, he replied with what "what are you going to do about it"? Sometimes Bob had a very short fuse, so he dived at the guy and the fight began. We were trying to get control of him, no punches being thrown; it was more like a wrestling match. We were in the street, on the sidewalk and in the grass. He was a very strong man and had very muscular arms; he was cussing and yelling the entire time. We wanted to get him down to handcuff him, when we finally got him down he had both arms spread out, I put one side of a handcuff on one arm, and both of us were trying to get his arms together so we could get the handcuffs together. He was so strong that we could not get his arms together, so we stood him up and somehow Bob got around being him, I had enough of this so I pulled out my blackjack and was going to give him a little tap on his jaw to stun him. When I swung the jack at his jaw, he tilted his head aside and I hit Cass in the eye. He let go of the guy and reminded me that his is on my team. Finally the guy says, let's stop this, walked over to the cruiser, got in the backseat and we took him to jail.

Another time it was real quiet on the East end, and we had just finished checking our district for the first time when we saw some fire trucks heading north on Cedar Street. I wanted to see where they were going, so we did. Much to our regret, this was a house fire on Ridge Avenue, when we got there the house was completely in flames and we watched the firemen fighting the fire, but it was completely gone. A fireman told us there was a body inside and the house was completely consumed. You could see the burned body laying there and the Fire Chief asked if we could go get the Coroner. He lived on North 5th Street, so we went and picked up Doctor Koehler and took him to the scene. When we got there the doctor asked Cass and I to go in there and drag the body out. Since the Coroner is always in charge of the scene where a dead body is found, we obeyed his order and went in and drug the body out of the house. The stench was all over our uniforms, and an ambulance was called and the body was taken to the rear of Criss Bros Funeral Home, where the Doc performed an autopsy and we had to go watch it. This was a gristly night, and we had a heck of a time getting that stench out of our uniforms. Let me tell you, we never followed a fire truck after that.

About a month after the fight we had on Market Street, we started out of the station around midnight. We had just turned onto the Canal Street alley, when we saw a woman lying in the alley. We got out and found that it was one of our local drunk females, passed out. To be safe we called for an ambulance, and had her taken to the hospital. That was on Everett Avenue, and at that time we followed the ambulance to the hospital. When we got there she was put onto a gurney and taken to a room. We went in the room with her, and Nurse Rolland came in, she was a very funny woman, and she checked out the patient. She was okay, just a few bruises from the fall. Bob then started to question her, what her name was and she had him confused with someone else and said you know my name we lived together for a long time. He said again, what is your name, and she said you know me Chuck. Nurse Rolland and I picked it up and started calling him Chuck. She then gave us the clearance to take her, so we put her in the cruiser and took her to the station. We wrote her up, telling her she was under arrest for drunkenness. The woman inmates were kept at the County Jail. So we took her there, she was written up and the woman inmates were kept on the 4th floor, so we were waiting on an elevator to come down and I said to her, you know that Chuck is a dirty no good, and she said your right. She then took her fist and hit Bob in the other eye. The elevator door opened and he was so mad he threw her onto the elevator. We had to go to the 4th floor and turn her over to the Matron. When we got out of the jail, Bob said to me, I am going to quit working with you before you get me killed. All I did was laugh and he had that shiner for a long time.

March 10th we got a call to go to my home, when we got there my wife was in labor. So we took her to the hospital in the cruiser. It was only 4 blocks away, I got off duty to be with her. On March 11th, 1952 Karen Cecile Fournier was born, a very cute little girl. I regret that I have to say this but I was doing wrong things. I was drinking, carousing with my friends ever chance I got and you would think that after seeing that all my life I wouldn't do it. But I did. It was very wrong, and looking back on that I really feel bad and sad that it happened. Eleanor was a good person, and loved her children. It was all me, all I wanted to do was have fun. I was very selfish. I never did anything wrong when I was working, it was always off duty stuff. My relationship with my wife was going downhill fast, and she was becoming nasty and crabby. I cannot blame her, it was my fault. I had enough, I was on inactive duty in the Naval Reserve, and the Korean War was going on. So I requested active duty in the Navy. I told the Chief that I was going on active duty and I resigned from the Police Department, the job I really loved.

I had moved my family to a little house on North 23rd Street and told my wife that I had requested for active duty in the Navy. I was to report to Philadelphia Naval Base in Pennsylvania by June 24th, 1952. I left in my 1948 Cadillac, arrived at the Naval Base on June 23rd and was assigned to be sent to Norfolk Naval Base in Virginia. I drove there and was sent to barracks to wait for a hip that I was to be assigned too. I waited for 2 weeks and was assigned to the Franklin D. Roosevelt, the largest Aircraft Carrier that I had ever seen. I was put in the galley, when the Chief Petty Officer saw my record about being Jack of the Dust. He requested that I should be in charge of the food stores for the ship, so I was. I had a nice office, and had plenty of food stores for the galley. I was doing the same things I had done before, keeping food supplies on hand and ordering more when they got low.

We headed out to sea, this time on the Atlantic Ocean. We landed in a bay about 10 miles from Glasgow, Scotland. We were there for about a month and got to go to Glasgow on liberty about every night. We met some girls and went night clubbing and to movies. We had a good time, and nothing serious happened. We then left and went thought the Straits of Gibraltar, into the Mediterrian Sea. We stopped in Sicily, and were there for about 3 days. We were about to sail the whole Mediterranean Sea, we went to Taranto Italy then back to Cannes, France, then to Beirut, Lebanon, then to Athens, Greece and then back to France. We sailed all over the area and then we went to Weymouth, England. We spent a lot of time there and were in that area for about 10 months. We then sailed back to the states and arrived back in Norfolk VA Naval Base around the last part of April 1953. I was detached from active duty and went back home.

When we were out to sea, I really missed my family. I wrote my wife and asked if she would take me back if I would straighten out and not do the things I had done before. She wrote me and said we will be waiting for you when you get home. I left for home in my 1948 Cadillac and couldn't wait to get there. I arrived home on May 10th, 1953 and was welcomed home with opened arms. My mother came to stay with us and again helped us. We found a nice house on North

8th Street, that I could get for $500 down with the G.I. Bill. I could apply again because I had been in the service during the Korean War. My mother loaned us the $500 and we bought the house. We moved it and it was a large 3 bedroom house with a nice kitchen, large dining room and large living room. It was really nice. I stopped my drinking except for a beer or two every once in awhile. I went to the P.D. and talked with the Chief, there was a vacancy so I went to the Civil Service Commission and applied to be reinstated to the Police Department. I was accepted because of being in the service during the war. May 15, 1953 I was a Newark Police Officer again, back to the job I really loved.

I was assigned to the north side walking beat from 12 midnight to 8am shift. It hadn't changed a bit, very quiet and we had to check all the local businesses. We had no walkie talkies; all we had to make contact with the station was the call boxes. If you found a place unlocked or open, whatever the case, you would go inside, check the place out and find a phone and call the station, they would then call the owner or manager and they would come down and lock up. I don't remember how many windows I climbed into to get into stores. It was so quiet on that beat that I started going up on roofs and into basements just to have something to do. We had to report to the station every hour on different call boxes.

One morning around 1am, there was a fire escape on the West side of the Midland Theater. I went up to the roof and you could see the whole downtown up there. That roof led to other roofs, west to an alley just before I got to the alley; there was a 12 foot opening. Down behind the Alibi Room, where they kept their trash, I almost fell down into that opening. It would have been quite a drop if I would have fallen. Down in that opening was a door leading to the alley

The Trials and Triumphs

that was locked. I tell you this because years later it came back to my memory when an incident happened.

One night when I was walking on the North side of the square, walking east, checking my business places, I went into an alley to check the rear of Cussin and Fearn Store. I pushed on the door, and it came open. I went inside and in the middle of the store I found a safe on a 2 wheel cart. I called the station and they sent a cruiser, there had been a break in and there must have been a lookout who warned them I was coming so they left the safe in the middle of the store and took off.

April 7, 1954 I came into the station around 6am to feed the prisoners and when I was done I was standing in the radio room, talking to Art Nutter Jr. We heard on the radio of a shooting in Johnstown, where a man shot and killed his stepfather. He was driving a green car with a ZZ license plate on it. Just then Art said there goes a car with a ZZ license plate on it, it headed south bound by the station and I said do you want me to check it out? All we had was a plain car, so Art gave me the keys and the traffic light had stopped the car so I pulled out and he was going through the light, and he turned in an alley headed East bound. He was headed toward 3rd Street where the County Jail and I thought he was going to the jail but he turned South bound on 3rd Street and was heading toward National Drive. There was a car between him and me, I had called for a cruiser and Roy Waldren and Jim Nichols were headed south bound on South 4th Street. The car turned onto National Drive, toward 4th Street, and the subject stopped at the stop sign, I pulled up behind him and told him to get out of the car. He slid over to the passenger side of the car, opened the door and got out. I told him to put his hands on top of the car and he did. By the time Roy and Jim got there, they came over and searched the car for a weapon, there wasn't one. I always seemed to take charge of things. So I said one of you drive his car to the station, and put him in my car and take him to the station. We handcuffed him behind his back and headed for the station. I asked him why he shot his stepfather, and he said that he was always picking on him; he had enough and got his revolver and killed him. We got to the station and called the Sheriff's Office and told them we had their suspect in the shooting in Johnstown. Jim and I went out and searched his car again and on the passenger's side we found a 32 revolver between the door and the seat. It was empty. We brought it into the station, and by that time Sheriff McElroy had arrived and too his prisoner and the gun to the County Jail. He didn't even say thank you. I tell you I admired Sheriff McElroy, he was the best sheriff that we ever had.

That was my second murder case. I had to go to court to testify and the statement about him having planned for awhile to kill his stepfather was what convicted him. He was sent to prison for life. This was another article for the scrapbook.

September 1954 we were assigned to the South and West cruiser district from 4pm to 12 midnight. Bob and I were a good team, we got involved with the usual fights and accidents and domestics. Feb.1, 1955 Bob was off sick and I was working with Hubert Cochenour. We got a call that someone was in the filling station on Hudson Ave and St. Clair Street. We arrived at the scene and Hubie went around to the back, I went to the front door and looked inside to see two men hiding behind the desk. I hollered at them to come out and they did, the front door was locked and they unlocked it and let me in, they were 12 and 14 year old boys. I called Hubie who was coming thru the window they had broken out. We took them into custody and I checked behind the desk and there were two pellet guns on the floor. We had the station call the owner of the gas station and when he arrived we took the two boys to the department. They confessed to breaking into other places, where they had stolen the pellet guns. They were charged with breaking and entering and went to juvenile court. They were good kids, very polite and obeyed our commands. They were brothers who lived with their grandfather and we took them to the County Jail. When they went to court, we went to bat for them and they were given probation. Oddly enough, year's later one of the boy's sons became a Police Officer and worked for me. I asked him if he knew those boys because he had the same last name, he said that was my father and uncle, and got a good laugh when I told him about it. As far as I know he is still on the Department and is a Sergeant.

February 14th, 1955 a call went out to the other cruiser that there was a shooting on Hollander Street. Cass and I were sent as backup and we arrived at the scene before the other cruisers, we found Rev. Starlie Brooks, who was a Pastor of a church on Hollander Street, he was lying on the back porch of his house and the squad was there. I leaned down and asked him who did this, and he said Homer, who was his son. I knew Homer because the week before I had got a call to the house and Homer had come home drunk and threatened the Reverend and his wife with a shotgun. We arrested Homer and took him to jail, we arrested him for drunkenness and he got out the next day at that time. I told the Reverend that he ought to take all his guns to Lester Hall's house as he lived around the corner from the reverend. But he didn't do that. I asked him where Homer had gone, and he said next door. The other cruiser arrived, so Cass and I went next door to talk to the neighbor. We were told that Homer asked him for a ride downtown, and he declined. So Homer left and walked to the Little Bear Store on Hudson Avenue. We got in our cruiser and went to Channel Street and turned onto Hudson and stopped at the Little Bear. Homer had gone into the store to call for a cab, as we stopped out of the store came Homer, I think he thought we were the cab, he started towards us and we jumped out of the cruiser, grabbed him and searched him, handcuffed him and put him in the cruiser and took him to the station. On the way to the station the other cruiser informed us the Reverend had died and Homer was sent to prison for life.

In March 1955 there were some big changes in the Police Department. Chief Christman had retired and Arthur (Deacon) Jones became Chief of Police. I will explain the promotion process, you had to be in rank for one year to be able to take a Civil Service Test for the next higher rank, it was a written examination and had to be competitive, two or more persons could take the test, the one with the highest promoted. Captain Ralph Hunter retired and the sergeants took the test for Chief of Detectives. Sergeant Lester Hall became Chief of Detectives, and Sergeant Bernard Howarth became Captain. The Newark City Council had approved to enlarge our Detective Division and approved 2 Lieutenants of Detectives and one Sergeant of Detectives and that test was open to Patrolmen. Charles Spurgeon and Bernard Coulter became Lieutenants of Detectives and Paul Lytle became Sergeant of Detectives. That left 2 desk Sergeants positions open, I took the test and passed. I became 12 midnight to 8am Desk Sergeant. George Campbell became the 4pm to 12 midnight Desk Sergeant and this was in May 1955.

The desk sergeant was like a dispatcher, receiving incoming calls and sending cruisers to different calls. I was in charge of records, and of the jail. I would take bonds for release of prisoners and take care of people who would come into the jail for help and is in 2nd command of the shift. About 4 months later, City Council approved the hiring of 2 Captains. The test was open to Patrolmen and Arthur Nutter Jr became the 4pm to 12 midnight shift Captain, and Hoy Cates became the 12 midnight to 8am shift Captain. Hoy and I had a good working relationship and I worked in that position for six years.

When I was desk sergeant, one morning about 3am a lady called the station and told me that she was going to kill herself, she wouldn't give her name, she just said that she was a Doctor's wife and that she was always alone. She was lonely and very depressed. I talked with her and tried to console her and I told her that if she did this she could not take it back. I told her she needed to pray and look at the bright things that had happened in her life. A call came in, so I told her to hold on and answered the call and got back to her and we talked until 6am. That time she said you have convinced me not to do this. She was not going to kill herself and she thanked me and hung up. I felt great knowing that may have helped someone from killing themselves.

January 1956, I was at the desk in the Radio Room and there was a large window on my right side, it was freezing cold. Around 3am I saw someone run by the window and come in the door, they came to the counter and I saw it was a woman. All she had on was a slip, barefooted and asked me to help her. She said her husband tried to flush her head in the commode, it struck me as funny. I began to laugh and I was laughing uncontrollably, she told me that it wasn't funny. I was laughing so much, that I had a hard time getting to the radio to call a cruiser in. I was able to compose myself, and grabbed my pea coat and put it around her shoulders. The cruiser came in and I told them they had to help her and that her husband tried to flush her head down the commode. They all started to laugh and I started to laugh again and she started to laugh this time. She told us that her husband had been to a party and they were drinking, when they got home they had a fight and he grabbed her by the hair, pulled her into the bathroom and put her head in the commode, the flushed it she got scared and ran out, she ran 8 blocks to the department and was shivering because it was below zero outside. I had the cruiser take her home and reminded her to bring my coat back. When they got to her home, her husband became lovey dovey and the cruiser left. I thought that was so funny.

There were some changes in our department and Chief Jones retired, so Lester Hall became the Chief of Police. The test was opened to the Captains and only one signed up so then it became open to two Lieutenants, Charles Spurgeon became Chief of Detectives. While he was lieutenant I would stay over after 8am and he would show me photography, dark room procedures and dusting for prints. It was very interesting and I enjoyed learning this. I would stay over whenever Charlie had the time to show me these things. About the first part of September 1956, Chief Hall sent Det. Sgt Paul Lytle and me to the Bureau of Criminal Identification and Investigation in London, Ohio for a 2 week course. It was enjoyable and I learned a lot. When the course was completed we got a diploma and came home, back to the 12 midnight to 8am desk. Paul Lytle became Lieutenant of Detectives; Sgt of Detectives position was open. So Chief Hall asked Charlie who wanted to fill that position and he asked for me, so I was transferred into the Detective Division as Sergeant of Detectives. I did all the crime scene searches and also assisted on investigation of felonies. I was teamed up with Paul Lytle, the bad part of the job was that you were called out at all hours of the night but I enjoyed it.

On July 25, 1958 Joseph Raymond Fournier was born, a real cute little boy. I now had 2 sons and a daughter. Every vacation we went someplace but mostly to New Jersey, Aunt Cecile and Uncle Stan had a house about 4 blocks from the ocean. We went there every day and really enjoyed ourselves. I loved my family and enjoyed being with them, we had a lot of fun together as they were growing up.

The Trials and Triumphs

Ned Ashton became the 12m to 8am desk Sgt. This was the makeup of our department and it was May 1961. Lester Hall was the Chief of Police, Charles Spurgeon was Chief of Detectives, Bernard Howarth was Captain 8 am to 4pm, Art Nutter was Captain 4pm to 12m, Hoy Cates was Captain 12m to 8am, Bernard Coulter was Lieutenant of Detectives, and Paul Lytle was Lieutenant of Detectives. I was Sergeant of Detectives, Homer Comisford was 8am to 4pm Desk Sergeant, George Campbell was 4pm to 12m Desk Sgt, Ned Ashton was 12m to 8am Desk Sgt. And six more Patrolmen were added to our department. We had 40 patrolmen at that time.

In May 1961, Chief Hall sent me to the Bureau of Identification in London, Ohio for training in Fingerprint Sciences. It was a 3 week course and I really enjoyed it. I learned all about fingerprinting, how to dust for prints, how to lift them, how to photograph them, and how to pick out points for identification. I learned a lot, the instructor informed us to remember that fingerprints don't catch people, they just identify them. After training I got a diploma and came home. I not only did crime scene searches but worked on different cases. One day I worked with Bernard Coulter, I learned a lot from him. He was a very good interrogator, he was very skillful and I watched him and learned a lot about how to interrogate people. Most of the time suspects would confess to the crimes when he got done. We were working on a case where many safes had to be taken from business places; these were small safes, wheeled out on a cart. He had a suspect in mind named Hensel. We picked Hensel, brought him to the station and he was a hard one to get to talk. Bernard was so skillful and Hensel confessed told us where they dumped the safes. He implicated two more suspects, 3 safes were taken out of the city and dumped in a field. One safe was buried in a garage; we located all the safes and picked up the other two suspects. They also confessed and we charged them with breaking and entering. The other two subjects went to prison, but because Hensel helped us out, we requested that he get probation, which he did.

Another case I worked on was a breaking and entering at a Bakery on Mount Vernon Road. I went to the scene; someone had broken out the rear window, lifted the glass and got inside. There were four cans with lids on them under the counter in the back room, once can was pulled out and a lid removed, there was a bag of money inside with $400. The bag had been removed and the suspect climbed out the same window. I photographed the scene, dusted the broken glass for fingerprints and found some very good ones. The manager filed a report, and her last name sounded familiar, I asked her if she had a son and she said yes, his name was Jack. Well I knew Jack was running around with a not so good crowd. I got to the station and photographed the prints, enlarged them and picked out 18 points; I got Jacks prints out of the files and could not make any points from his prints. I knew he was running around with a man named Danny, so I pulled his file and got his prints and figured out that Danny was the one that had got into the bakery. I picked Danny up and showed him the points I had picked that showed it was him that committed the crime. As much as I tried, he would not confess. I charged him with breaking and entering, we went to court and he was convicted and sent to prison. And I proved fingerprints not only identify people, they also catch them.

I worked a lot of cases where fingerprints were found. I was in court all the time testifying. One day I was testifying in a case and the Defense Attorney was new and was trying to trip me up. Judge Bolton interrupted him and said we all know that Sgt Fournier is a fingerprint expert, so there is no need to do any further questioning. How do you become a fingerprint expert? By studying, working a lot on cases, schooling, and one other thing, Judicial Notice. When Judge Bolton claimed I was a fingerprint expert, I never did have any more problems with attorneys.

Around October 1961, Chief Hall sent me again to London, Ohio for training in Handwriting and Questioned Documents. It was a 2 week course and I got another diploma and came back home. Chet White and Don Norris were assigned to the Detective Division as Patrolmen Detectives. I was assigned to work with Chet White. Lieutenant Paul Lytle retired and all the Sgts were allowed to take the test for Lieutenant. I came out first on the test and as appointed to Lt. of Detectives. In April 1964, Chet White became Sgt. of Detective. I always loved sports, and was a big OSU fan since I was 11 years old. I began coaching Little League baseball, football and Biddy Basketball. I played basketball on the American Legion Team and we started a basketball team at the Police Department. I played on that team and played softball for Marcel Potato Chip Company and on the Police Department softball team. I was quite busy but did not do it all at the same time.

Chet and I worked well together, although he did something that was not appropriate. We were having a lot of breaking and entering in the city. Moore's Stores and other large stores where guns, televisions or other large items were being taken. And we were having trouble getting leads on this. One day Deputy Bill Belter came to the department and told Chief Spurgeon that he might have a lead for us. He said that Jim was running this gang and I knew Jim because I had arrested him before for thefts. Belter and Jim had a barbershop in Thornville; he told us where it was. In the meantime 2 detectives from Whitehall, just outside of Columbus, had a break in at the Union Store where furs and jewelry were taken. Chet and I along with 2 Whitehall Detectives headed for Thornville. It was 7:30pm when we got to the Babar shop, just as Jim was closing. We went inside and I had always treated Jim decently when I had arrested him before, I talked to him about the entire break ins and I told him we had evidence that he was involved. To my surprise, he told me he was running the operation. Two other guys, John and Jim, were on their way to Newark at this time with a carload of furs and jewelry. They were going to meet someone behind the Newark Trust Company and sell it. The Newark Trust was right in front of the department and there was a large parking lot in between. I called the department and alerted them about this car. The Whitehall Detective left and we loaded Jim in the plain car and headed to Newark, in the meantime we got word on the radio that the car with John was in custody. On the way to Newark, Jim asked if we could stop at his trailer in Heath so he could say goodbye to his wife and kids. He knew that he was going to prison because he was on probation for other thefts. So we took him to his home, we went inside with him and identified ourselves to his wife and told her what happened. He kissed her and the kids and said goodbye. We left for the department, and when we got there took him to our office and talked with him. He told us all the places he had broken into and it totaled about $30,000 worth of merchandise, large quantities of televisions, guns and other items. He told us how much he would resell the items for and who too. One of the men lived in Crooksville and he bought a lot of Jim's merchandise. We got his name along with the others and picked them all up and charged them with receiving stolen property. We worked on this case for 18 hours and the next day Chief Spurgeon and Chet and I got a truck and went to Crooksville. We located this man's house, and next door was an empty store. He took us to the store and I couldn't believe how much merchandise he had in that store, it was packed with all the stolen merchandise. We loaded it in the truck, took him into custody and headed for Newark. We stored the merchandise and locked Mr. Reed in jail, charging him with receiving stolen merchandise. All told with the furs and jewelry which amounted to $12,000 and the other items to about $40,000. Chet and I got our pictures in the newspaper, didn't get paid for overtime but the paper showed Chief Spurgeon giving us a large lollipop for our good job. That is also in my scrapbook. Jim and John were sent to prison and the others received probation.

    I have to tell you the story about this young man I dealt with and about the things that he got involved with. I will call him Freddie. I first got involved with him when he was 15 years old. The Athanor Heating and Cooling Office were broken into in 1963. I did the crime scene search and found that fire had been set to papers in a 2 tier wire basket, also to papers on the desk; the suspect was looking for money. Not finding any he set a fire, the Fire Department was called and there wasn't too much damage. We received information that a boy had broken in by the name of Freddie. We found where he lived and picked him up; we took him to the department and questioned him. At first he wouldn't say anything but I became very friendly and talked to him about his life and got him a can of pop. He became very talkative and there was a feeling between us that drew us closer together. I told him I would try to help him, if I could. He was a very nice young man; I took a liking to him. And I got the feeling that he liked me and trusted me too. I asked him again about the break in and he said that he did it and set the fire because he could not find any money. I went to bat for him in Juvenile Court and he got probation. Freddie was always getting into trouble; he was arrested again for theft. He got sentenced to a Boys Industrial School in Lancaster. In May 1967, Chet and I were investigating a break in at Chesrown Olds on East Main Street; two new cars had been stolen from their garage. Once car was found wrecked on Riverside Drive and the other was found on High Street abandoned. We had no clues as to who had done this. I dusted the cars and never came up with any prints. One day I spotted Freddie walking down the street, Chet and I were driving on Mt. Vernon Road two or three days later. I told Chet that Freddie must have walked away from Lancaster. So we stopped and picked him up, we took him to the department and questioned him about leaving the school and he said he had been released a week earlier. We asked him if he had something to do with the Chesrown break ins and he said he didn't do it. I told him to empty his pockets and put it all on the table; low and behold he had two new sets of keys in his pocket. I said what about those? And he confessed to the break in and stealing the cars. He went to court and was sentenced to Orient Prison at 19 years old.

The neighborhood on North 8th Street was getting run down with undesirable people moving in there. So we sold out house and bought a nice 3 bedroom house in the North end of town on Kenarbre Drive. We like it very much, that was in 1965.

There were more changes in the department in 1966. Captain Bernard Howarth retired and Ned Ashton became Captain of the 12m to 8am shift. Captain Roy Cates moved to the 4pm to 12m shift and Captain Art Nutter Jr. became Captain of the 8am to 4pm shift. Bill Comisford became Sgt of Detectives and in July 1968, Chief Hall retired. Charles Spurgeon became Chief of Police and in September 1968 Ned Ashton became Chief of Detectives and left a captains position open.

July 11, 1968 we received a call of an armed robbery at Forkers Café on Union Street. The cruiser was there taking a report and Sgt Comisford, Bob Cass and I went to the scene. We talked to witnesses and were informed that a man with a pistol came in and said to give him all the money. He was given about $3,400 and ran out and jumped into a car and there was another man and woman in the car too. We got the

The Trials and Triumphs

description of the car from a patron and as she was telling us about it, a man came in and said he heard her and that was his car. He had loaned it to a man named John and that Buck and Patty were with him. I asked where they lived and he said that they told him when they borrowed the car they were going to Patty's apartment in Columbus. I got Patty's address, and seeing as though the Chief was on vacation and I was the oldest Lieutenant, I made the decision that Bob, Bill and I would head for the apartment in Columbus. When we got to her apartment, her roommate answered the door and we identified ourselves, she let us in and told us that Patty was not there. And that she had left with 2 men about an hour previous and she generally hung out at bars in the North end. Since we were in Columbus Police jurisdiction, I called them and told them our circumstances and asked if a couple of detectives could join our search for the 3 suspects. I knew John, Buck and Patty as I had arrested them before on minor charges. The detectives arrived and we started checking all the bars in the North End. There sure were a lot of bars in that area and we couldn't locate them. So we drove downtown and parked across from the Greyhound Bus Station and the Columbus officers said they were going off duty and left. We went into the bus station and could not find them, and checked with a clerk to see if they had recognized them and were told no. We believed we were at a dead end, so we left the bus station and had to wait for a red light to change to cross the street, just as the light changed and we were getting ready to cross, a cab pulls up and stops, and out of the cab comes John, Buck and Patty. Right in front of us and we took them into custody. Buck took off running but Bill Comisford caught him and brought him back. We loaded them all into our car and headed to Newark. On the way Patty had a purse on her lap, and I took it and looked in it and found a pistol and $2,900 in cash. We got to the department and put them in separate rooms. I had Patty, Bill had

The Trials and Triumphs

John and Bob had Buck. I told Patty if she would cooperate with me and testify against the other two, I would try and get her probation. She did and wrote me a statement as to what happened and referred the armed robbery. John and Buck wouldn't say a word. I went to the prosecutor and advised him that Patty had cooperated and gave him her statement. John and Buck were tried and convicted of armed robbery and sentenced to 5 years in prison. Patty was charged with complicity and put on probation. A few years later I saw her at a store and she came up and hugged and thanked me for getting her that probation.

There were a lot more changes in the Police Department. They made 3 more Sergeants, added 6 more Patrolmen and the Captain vacancy. Chief Spurgeon called me into his office and asked me if I would take charge of the 12m to 8am shift, just until a Captains Test was given. I said I would, so I was assigned to the 12m to 8am shift, back in uniform and had to buy Lieutenant Bars for my uniform shirt. At the time some Patrolmen were put in the radio room as dispatchers and the Sgts were put on patrol. Some Patrolmen also worked the records room, the 12m shift had one dispatcher and one records clerk, and 10 patrol officers, 2 Sgts., and 1 Lieutenant in command. They also added 1 more cruiser and had 3 walking beats downtown.

December 11, 1968, they gave the Captains Test, Chet White and I took the test. Chet had a photographic memory, and I thought he was going to be hard to beat on the test. The night of the test, which was given in an office at the department, we took the test and they graded them after we both finished. We waited, and I was called into the office and told that I got the highest grade and would be promoted to Captain. I was very excited and went home and told my wife and kids. The next day I was sworn in as Captain of Police of the Newark Police Department. I was assigned to the 12m to 8am shift. When we reported to give muster (reporting for duty, given assignments, and find out what happened on the previous 2 shifts) that day, we were supposed to be on station 15 minutes before 12m. When I came in that night, my men came forward and gave me Captains Bars for my shirt collar and for my shoulders. I still have these to this day.

Let me tell you about the men on this shift, many did not show any enthusiasm, they would just report for duty, they didn't put out. I had two men, Gene Thompson and Larry Powell, they were go getters. An example of this was when they mounted a tape recorder in the trunk of their cruiser with a mike in the backseat. When they arrested a couple suspects, in a theft or break in, they would put them in the back seat and walk away to let them talk to each other. It would all be recorded on tape, incriminating them. When they got to the station they would play the tape to the suspects and they would confess.

I was determined to change the attitudes of the men. So at muster time, I would call Gene and Larry to the front and commend them for the great job that they did. So when other officers would do a good job, I would call them up and commend them also. The men really perked up and really started putting out the work. Before long everyone on the shift was doing a great job and they were making a lot of felony and traffic arrests. Everyone had a great attitude and we all worked well together. On major calls I would go out on the scene with them, in case they had a question that they couldn't figure out. They liked that, and I was gaining a lot of respect from them.

September 1969, we received a teletype of a wanted person in Toledo. He was wanted for Auto Theft, his name was Floyd. I knew Floyd, as I had arrested him before. A description of the car was put, but I knew where Floyd lived, with his parents just off East Church Street. I sent a cruiser and I went myself, since I knew him. When we got to his house there was a stolen car sitting there, so I called for another cruiser. When they got there I had them watch the outside of the house and the other officers and I went to the door. Floyd's dad opened the door and I asked if Floyd was there. His dad said that he wasn't there but offered to let us come in and search the house, so we searched all the rooms. As I was coming out of the bedroom, I looked up and saw a trap door ajar, which led to the attic. I got a chair and lifted the trap door and could see someone inside. It was dark and all I saw was a shadow, so I said Floyd, come down, with no answer. We sprayed mace up there but there was no movement, so I told my men I was going to the station to get some tear gas. Floyd heard this and ended up coming down. We took him into custody and took him to the department, then called the Toledo Police Department and they came and got him.

October 1959, we heard on the radio that Heath Police cruisers were chasing a truck that was involved with several breaking and entering in New Lexington and Heath. The truck was loaded with stolen merchandise, and there were 5 men in the truck. As the Heath cruisers were chasing them, the suspects were throwing articles of stolen merchandise out of the truck into the officer's path. We were in contact with the officers and they said they were entering Newark and headed West on Church Street. My three cruisers and myself in a cruiser headed for the area. One cruiser was headed South on 13th and one headed East on Church Street. We saw the truck and he had evidentially seen our cruisers, so he turned north on 13th Street and we had him cornered. They stopped the truck and all 5 suspects jumped out and started to run. We caught 2 in the bushes behind the YMCA, and the other 3 were in the area, it was dark and they were said to be armed. I pulled my men back and we cordoned the area, to wait till it got light out. Men from the 8am shift came in and we searched the whole area, eventually the 3 men were captured and the whole department got a nice write up in the newspaper. That is in my scrapbook, along with a lot of other things.

Chief Spurgeon called all the Captains and the Chief of Detectives into his office and said we are going to make some changes. Charlie was an avid reader of anything concerning Police matters and said he was going to change the Captains jobs, one Captain will be in charge of the Patrol Division, one in charge of Records and Communications, and one in charge of all Administrative work. Nutter Jr will be in charge of Patrol Division, Cates will be in charge of Records and Communications Division, and Fournier would be in charge of Administrative Officer. The change was effectively immediately, and this was in May 1970.

I had said to myself, what does Administrative Officer do? I soon found out. I was in charge of writing, rules and procedures, budgeting for the Department, writing rules and procedures, budgeting for the Department Training, investigating charges against officers, assisting the Chief on different matters and I found myself very busy but I liked it.

One day the Chief told me that we were going to Cambridge Police Department to see their Community Police Relations Division and how they got funding from the Federal Government. Charlie was interested in having a Community Relation Bureau in our department. We went to Cambridge and they showed us their bureau and gave us paperwork on how we could apply. The next day the Chief said we were going to Worthington Police Department to see about their Community Relations Bureau, which we did. It was very interesting and on the way back to Newark he asked me to write up a program and application to the State Bureau of Federal Funding in Columbus, so we would get federal funding for a bureau in our department. I told him I would try. The Chief went to Major Richard Baker and to Council with the idea; it would not cost the city anything but for two officer's salary which would be in kind funds. It was approved by both the City Council and the Major. I put an application to the State Bureau for a $32,300 grant. We had a man by the name of Jack Lawry, who worked for the State Narcotics Bureau who used to stop into our department and I got well acquainted with him when I was in the Detective Division, little did I know that Jack had been transferred, and as the one who approved all Federal Funding request and granted ours.

Chief Spurgeon told me that it would be my job to run the Community Relations Bureau. I was assigned two officers and a Secretary, I had quite a large office and there was room in there. Barbara Brown was appointed as our Secretary and Chief asked me who I wanted as the 2 officers. About a year before my best friend from Buckeye Lake days had gotten on the force, Russ Yontz. When he was a kid he was always a great talker and had a very good disposition and was always smiling and laughing. So I picked Russ and then I picked Tom Francis, who was the same way. I wanted someone like that because they would be sent out to different groups and organizations to give talks to them about our department and our goals. The purpose of our program would be to acquaint citizens with the operations, practices and policies of the Police Department and to acquaint the Police Department with the various problems the citizens had.

I put out a directive to the Department that if any officer had any ideas of programs to let me know. Russ, Tom, Barbara and I got our heads together and started planning programs for the Police Community Relations Division. We had just gotten together when Patrol Bill Queen comes in the office and said I have a program for you if you want to use it. We had a rash of women being assaulted in the city. Bill and

The Trials and Triumphs

I know Judo and Karate, how about a self defense class for woman? I thought it was a great idea, so we worked it out on how we could do this. Bill had a woman who would volunteer to assist him and she was also into Karate and Judo.

The women were taught fitness, exercise and points of attacks. They were also told how to avoid situations that could make it easier for them to be attacked. Each class attuned 4 weekly, 2 hour sessions to learn self defense combing forms of Judo and Karate. Each class had 24 members because of the space in the Police Department Squad room was limited. The program took off. We advertised it in the paper and many women signed up for the classes. We started in April 1972 and had classes booked clear to September. It was a very popular with the women and we continued this to 1973, and always had a full class.

In May 1972, we started a county wide Shoplifting Clinic. Jerry Garmen, of the State Adult Education Program, out on this program and there were about 100 store owners and managers at the clinic, it was held at Owens Corning Club House on Hollander Street. They were shown how to spot shoplifters, how to guard against shoppers who would linger near counters and never buy anything, how to spot hiding places of stolen merchandise; such as fake boxes, large shopping bags, and umbrellas. It was an excellent clinic and very successful.

We instructed women how to stop a Peeping Tom. Told them to have all doors locked, pull your shades, and before answering the door check to see if the person is a stranger. Women doing household chores should not wear clothes which could invite a Tom. And in May 1972, I had 4 Newark Catholic High School students come to my office, advising me they would like to teach younger students about the evils of drugs. I talked with them and it seemed like a real good program. They sure did know about the bad drug situation. We set the program up for 7th and 8th graders and went to the

The Trials and Triumphs

auditorium of the schools and the students putting on the class would ask for questions. Some of the questions were, can you get high on peanut butter if it is injected in your veins? What are fire trucks and footballs? When can a flashback occur? They also asked about the different kinds of drugs and about the hazards of drugs. I was surprised at the questions, but was doubly surprised that the students were able to answer them. This was a very educational program and we went to a lot of Junior High Schools with it.

I received a call from State Farm Insurance Company and was informed that they wanted to get involved with a program where people could engrave their social security numbers on all there large items in their homes. State Farm would provide electric pens for the engraving, and it didn't have to be by their social security number, and identifying number could be used. They gave us 10 pens and citizens had 3 days to use them and return them to the department. We then would give them a Project Theft Guard sticker for their front door. This proved to be very successful and many people would come and get the pens to use them. There were 3 good reasons why theft guard would help fight burglaries, 1. Fences who buy and sell stolen merchandise do not like to deal with stolen merchandise that could easily be identified. 2. The thief would think twice before being caught with stolen goods with engraved numbers on them and 3. The engraved numbers would have to be filed off or erased off, making it harder for burglars.

Russ and Tom would go out and talk to groups, organizations and schools. Barbara would schedule them and they were doing a fantastic job. We made a sound slide program on a projector and took pictures of all the areas of the department so we could take it anywhere and give a tour of the department. Next we went out and made a Bicycle Safety Program on the sound slide projector. Russ and Tom toured the city taking pictures showing safe and unsafe practices on riding and bike safety. The kids really enjoyed getting involved with that and when completed it was shown at schools and organizations. We included other programs such as safety tops for babysitters, we organized neighborhoods to have people observe while the owner was away.

We were very busy, and even gave tours to groups who came to the department to see it. We had our Community Relations Vehicle in the underground garage and it was equipped like the other cruisers, lights and siren, radio, etc. We would let the kids get behind the wheel of the car and they really liked that. A Safety Committee was set up of 4 business owners or managers and me. We would meet every month to discuss ways to promote safety on the city streets. The next year, 1973, we got a $21,000 grant for our Bureau. We received a letter from Jack Lawry that we were becoming one of the best Community Relations Bureau's in the State. Many people from different departments would come to see our operations and we got a letter from the Steubenville Police Department that they were deeply impressed with our setup. We got an award from the Optimist Club for our Bureau. One day, Paul Ripko, the manager of the AAA said we had been invited to the Columbus Convention Center, as the Governor was going to be there. Little did I know that they Committee had put me up for an award, and there were over 200 people there, the Governor, John Gilligan and another man came on the stage and were handing out awards. I heard Captain Robert Fournier of the Newark Police Department please come to the stage, I went up and received a nice plaque from Governor Gilligan. It was for the best Traffic Safety Program in the state of Ohio, for the bicycle program we had set up earlier. I was both proud and humbled. I thanked the Governor and went back and sat down. I was proud because Russ and Tom had worked so hard putting that program together and humbled because we had received such a nice award.

Around January 1973, the Chief called me into his office. He showed me a Police Magazine that he had been reading, and showed me an article about a department in a city in Arizona. I don't remember the name of the city but the department had gone to a 4/10 program for their department. That was working 4-10 hour days and having 3 days off. Chief had asked me to find out what I would about it and I got on the phone and called them. I asked about the program they had and asked if they could send me all the information about it. I had the information in about 3 days and started working on it. I was very difficult but I worked it out. We had very little training in our department, but I felt we needed more. So this is how I worked it out. There would be 6 teams with a Sgt in charge of the shift. We had 6 sgts and teams 1-3 and 5 would work Wednesday, Thursday and Friday and Saturday, and have Sunday, Monday and Tuesday off. Teams 2-4 and 6 would work Sunday, Monday, Tuesday and Wednesday and have Thursday, Friday and Saturday off. Since I had everyone working on Wednesdays, I would have a training program for teams 1-3-5 on the first Wednesday of each month, and the other team would be working. Then on the second Wednesday of each month I would have training for teams 2-4-6. Everyone got 10 hours of training every month, which amounted to 120 hours of training every year and the third Wednesday of each month, teams 1-3-5 would be off and teams 2-4-6 would work and on the fourth Wednesday, vice versa. I presented this to the Chief and he liked it and he called a staff meeting of the Captains and Chief of Detectives, we all went over it and everyone agreed that we should adopt it. The next thing was how the men would handle it. We had the Sgts go over it with the men on their shifts and it seemed like everyone liked it. So in March of 1973 we went to the 4/10 program. We had 8 patrolmen and one Sgt on each team, 1 patrolman worked in records, on as a Radio dispatcher and there were six cruiser patrolmen. The men loved it and everyone had a weekend day off.

Around June 1973, many of the men felt they were underpaid and were forced to take other jobs to support their families. We had several radicals in our department who had convinced about 30 men to have a sick out. I was starting my vacation, leaving the next day for New Jersey. My cousin Richard came to our house with his family and we were all going on vacation together. Around 10pm I got a call from the Chief and he told me to get my uniform on and get to the station, I reminded him I was leaving for vacation and he told me vacation was over. I got to the station he said that 30 people had marked off sick so all the rest of the men were put to 12 hour shifts and so was I. We worked from 9pm to 9am, and the next night I got to work around 10pm and got a call from home that a cross was burning in my yard, so I rushed home and found it still burning and put it out. I had an idea who might have done this, so I started for the Police Lodge in the West end of town to confront them. I was angry because my whole family was scared. As I started I got a call from the station that a bomb threat came in referenced to City Hall. The Police Department was in the basement of City Hall, but we couldn't find anything. I issued a statement to the press labeling the incident as childish and not likely to result in building and maintain a good public image that our Police Department wants and needs. And I appealed to the good, hard working officers to come back to work. Nine men reported back to work. Mayor Baker sent a letter to the remaining 21 officers that were off to report back to work or be fired. Several days passed and the remaining officers reported back.

Chief Charles Spurgeon retired in 1974 and a test was given for the Chief's position. Art Nutter, Roy Cates and I took the test. Nutter beat me by 3 points and took the position. He assigned me to be in charge of the Uniformed Police Division. Bob Post became Captain and was assigned as Administrative Officer. Cates was assigned to be in charge of Records and Communications Division. I was also Training Officer. We had a State Certified Police Academy and I became Commander of the Academy and was also an instructor we had 4 instructors, Bob Post, Bill Davis, and John Swick who was a Deputy Sheriff. We had people from all over the County coming to our school to become Police Officers.

When we had Patrolmen working as Dispatchers, I had a really nice young officer working the desk. He was very intelligent and outgoing. His name was James Dean, who we called Jimmy. His Grandfather had been a police officer by the name of Dewey Hayes. I had worked with Dewey when I became an officer and he was a very outgoing person and very funny. I tell you about Jimmy because later on in my life he became very important to me.

Another change that happened in the department was that they hired 3 civilians to work as Record Clerks in our department. They also hired 4 civilians to be Dispatchers and 2 meter maids that worked in our department. After working as Patrol Captain, I was transferred to Records and Communications Division and that was in 1976. Chief Nutter put the Captains back on 3 shifts and I took the 12m to 8am shift.

In April of 1976, a call came into the station that there was a large smell of gas in the air around the end of Webb Street. A cruiser was sent to the scene and I went also. In the railroad yards at the end of South Webb Street there were six large tank cars on the siding and the gas smell was large. The Fire Department was called when they got there; Assistant Chief Jim Lennon and I got together and decided that we would get up on the tank cars to locate the leak. We had our men get way back and I got on top of one tank car, while Jim on another. On top of the cars there were valves with wheels to shutoff gas. I found nothing on my car, so I went to the third car and heard a hissing sound. It was coming from the shutoff wheel and I could smell a heavy order of gas coming from it. I hollered to Jim that I found it and tried to turn it off but it would not turn. Jim got on top with me and tried to turn it, Jim had a medal on a chain around his neck and we were bent over trying to turn the wheel and the end of the medal was hitting it. I told Jim to take that medal off because one spark and we would be blown into the sky. He took it off and we turned the wheel and it finally started to turn. We applied more pressure and finally got it turned off. The gas stopped flooding the area and we got the Rail Road Company to pull the tank cars out of the city. A Railroad officer told us that if a spark or lighting had hit that leaking car, an area around 2,000 yards would have been leveled. I think we saved a lot of people; it was a potential time bomb.

Following that deed, Chief Nutter sent a letter to Safety Director Starr:

Dear Mr. Starr,
I would like to bring to your attention the
outstanding work performed but two members of
the Department of Public Safety,
Sunday morning, and April 18, 1976.
Captain Robert Fournier, Newark Division of Fire,
acted above and beyond the call of duty when the B
and O Railroad yard, no one else
in the United States would discuss the problem of
a leaking gas tank, did climb atop a tank car and
determined that a leak was in a valve,
and tightened the valve,
thereby eliminating the leak.

These actions, in a potentially dangerous situation, will only reflect on the Division of Police and Division of Fire.
Sincerely,
Arthur Nutter
Chief of Police

I thought that was very nice of Chief Nutter, for giving us that commendation.

On the home front, things were going along good. John had got married and left home as did Karen. And for some reason we had stopped going to church around 1965 after we moved on Kenarbe. Dr. Joe was 18 and still at home. We had good neighbors and we would get together taking turns at each other's houses, learning how to square dance. Fred Citrone and his wife, Gordon Carlson and his wife, Ken Gray and his wife are who we lived next door too and things were going good. In January of 1977, my wife got a job as a maid, in a big hotel at West Church and 2nd Street. Suddenly, things began to change. She became sullen and would hardly talk to me. Sometimes she was very nasty and I would ask her what the problem was and she wouldn't talk to me. I couldn't hug or kiss her and it wasn't long after that she moved me into Karen's room to sleep. I was always alone, and didn't know if she was going through a change in life or had another man. I knew I wasn't doing anything wrong, and I had been straight and narrow since getting back from the Navy in 1953. Around September of 1977, I had enough and packed my clothes and left. I got a rooming house on West Church Street and that's when I began doing wrong. But sometimes wrong things end up right. There was a very pretty meter maid, she was a nice person with a great personality and she was going through a divorce. She had 3 children and we started seeing each other, she was so pleasant. I enjoyed being with her. We would go for rides and we liked to talk to each other. Her divorce became final and she took me to her house to meet her kids. Steve was 9 years old, Stacy was 6 years old and Sean was 3 years old. Sean and Stacy took to me but Steve was laid back and wasn't sure of me. It wasn't long before he liked me too. I knew I was doing wrong, seeing another woman while being married, so about a month after I left home I went past the old house and saw a strange car in the driveway. Several nights later the car was there again, this was after midnight each time I saw it. I got a registration and found out it belonged to a man by the name of Anderson. I hired a private detective to check this out, and was informed the man was living there. Around January 1978, my wife filed for divorce and in February I was divorced. I was falling in love with Pam LeFever, and told her so. She was so nice, she took me to meet her mother and stepfather and they were very nice too. There was quite a difference in our ages, she was 28 and I just turned 51.

Pam and I were seeing each other about everyday now, and I had fallen in love with her. And she said she loved me too, then something happened that would change my life forever, Pam invited me to church, She attended the Maple Avenue Christian Union Church on Maple Avenue. We went to church on a Sunday around March 1978, we sat in a pew and many people came up and welcomed me to the church. There must have been 15 to 20 people that came over and I felt very welcomed, like I belonged there. It made me want to come back again. The Pastor Robert Carter began to preach; he was a very dynamic preacher and would give the message straight out of the Bible. I knew then that I would be coming back, we came to church every Sunday and Pastor Carter told us about our blessed Savior, Jesus Christ. I couldn't wait to come back to church. I had been a Catholic for most of my life, an Altar Boy for 9 years serving Mass, but for the first time in my life I began to understand about Jesus

Christ. How he loved us and died for us so our sins could be forgiven, simply by believing in him.

I asked Pam to marry me and she said yes, meeting her and marrying her made my whole life again. That was June 17, 1978. We were married by Pastor Carter in the Sanctuary of the Church and before we got married the Pastor met with us several times. He took the Bible and took me down the Roman Road; Romans 3:23, for all have sinned a come short of the Glory of God. Romans 6:23, For the Wages of sin is death, but the gift of God is eternal life through Jesus Christ our Lord. Romans 5:8, But God commended his love toward us, in that while we were yet sinners, Christ died for us. Romans 10:13, for whosoever shall call upon the name of the Lord shall be saved. The Pastor asked if I understood this, and I said yes, then he asked if I wanted to call on the Lord to be my personal Savior, and I said yes. He had me pray after him, and he led me on a prayer;

> Dear Heavenly Father,
> Thank you Jesus for saving me, I believe on your Holy name, I know that I am a sinner and I ask you for your forgiveness, Guide me and direct me in the way I should go, Help me to do my best for you each day and serve you the best that I can, I trust you to take me to Heaven when I die, I love you Lord and I praise your Holy Name,
> in Jesus name I pray.

After the wedding, we had a reception in the multi-purpose room of the church. Mostly relatives and friends from the church, Pam had 3 sisters; Judy, Linda and Sheila, their husbands and their children, all really nice people. After the reception we went on a honeymoon with our 3 children, we went to Cedar Point Amusement Park and stayed at the Holiday Inn. We went to the park several times, and then

Linda and Jim had a trailer on the shores of Lake Erie. We stayed there for several days.

I rented a big house on Mount Vernon Road; it had 4 bedrooms, a large living room with a fireplace, large dining room and a small kitchen. Each child had their own room. I really loved that house, it was nice and we lived there for 7 years. We continued to go to church and Sunday school ever week. We had been going to that church for about 2 months when Perry Jones asked me if I would be a Trustee. I agreed and was responsible for maintaining the church. The board meets every month and all board members are elected to their position every year. About a month later, Perry asked me if I would sit in on his Sunday school class. He taught 3rd, 4th and 5th grade boys, I enjoyed that. I was determined that I would serve the Lord in whatever he wanted me to do, whether it was small or large. Perry asked me if would take over his class, and I did. The next year I was voted in as 2nd Elder, I held that position for several years and then became 1st Elder and Sunday School Superintendent. I also had that position for several years and eventually went back to being 2nd Elder and taught Sunday school and sang in the choir. We began to go to all the services and when we started at Church, Sunday morning, Sunday night and Wednesday night. Pam became Sunday School Teacher and Assistant Director of Junior Church. We were very active and still are after 30 years. I drove the school van and picked up people and children for Sunday school and Church Service. I did that for about 16 years. At the present time I am an Elder; I open up the church every Sunday, unlock the doors, turn on the lights, and turn on the heat or air conditioner. I will do anything to serve my Lord. I moved the Church grass, shoveled snow and I am still committed to serving the Lord until I get old and infirmed. Then I will pray and read my Bible every day, My Daily Bread, and a book Pam gave me called Talking to the Lord. I served as 3rd Elder, taught Junior High Sunday school, had a puppet ministry with the Jr. High kids. I taught the High School Class, and at the present time I lead Bible Study at the church on Wednesday night. It gives me Joy to serve my Lord. That wonderful lady that I really loved, Katie Loughner, who was Director of Jr. Church, passed away and Pam became the Director. She has been serving in that position for 15 years and still teaches her Sunday Class. So you can see how my Savior and Lord, Jesus Christ, changed my life. I read many Christian books; my favorite was by Dr. John R. Rice. By reading these books, I was about to write 4 messages about Salvation. The last days, Hell and Heaven, which I presented to my Jr. High class, High school class, Young adult class and senior adult class. I prepare Communion for our church and serve Communion every month. I'm not telling you this for any credit; I want you to know how I serve the Lord and love it.

When I joined the church, Pastor Carter and I would go out every Tuesday evening and visit the sick of the church, or the widows or any house in our area. I would see him lead people to the Lord and hoped to do that same thing someday. We went to this man's house and his name was Orville Smith. We talked and the Pastor led him to the Lord. He was sickly and had to have oxygen and he prayed and accepted Jesus as his personal Savior. I felt sorry for him so every Thursday I would go visit him and we would talk. I told him that I was retired from the department and he told me that his son was on the Police Department now. He said his name was Tom Smith, and I told him that was one of my men when I was on the department. That drew us closer and we talked and read the Bible and had a closing prayer. I visited him for almost a year and one day I said Orville, why doing you say the closing prayer and he did. I was proud of him and it wasn't long after that he passed away. I knew he went to be with the Lord, and that I will seem him someday. While I was on the department I did lead 3 people to the Lord, using Roman

Road. They all prayed and accepted Jesus as their Personal Savior.

Now back to my job. In March 1980, Chief Nutter retired and became Safety Director, Bob Post, Hoy Cates and I took the test for that position. Post beat me on the test by 1 point, and became Chief. I was devastated because I really wanted to be Chief of Police. I lost heart and desire and since I had 30 years on the department, I decided to retire. I had been working part time for Jack Dunlap, who was a Police Officer, he had a Tarping Business and they put canvas tops on semi trucks. They carried mostly fiberglass, from Owens Corning and I became the foreman for Jack. I had 4 young men working for me and would go to the lot and put tarps on the fiberglass and with long straps tighten the tarps down. I did that for a year and some of the young men were unreliable and wouldn't show up for work, so I had to do the work myself. I asked Jack for a raise, he wouldn't give me one, so I quit.

We had a Police and Fire golf league that we would play on once a month. Bob Post was in the league and one day I was playing with him and we were talking about the department. He told me there was a vacancy in the Records Room as a clerk. I asked him if I applied, could I get the job and he would approve it, and he agreed. I applied and got the job, here I was back at the department working from 8am to 4pm, and little did I know that I would work there for 21 more years. I asked Pam to quit her meter maid job, I wanted to be the breadwinner in our family and she would have more time with the children. She did. I loved my wife with all my heart, and still do to this day. March 1989, Pam became pregnant and on December 16, 1989 Hannah Joy Fournier was born. What a pretty little girl, we had more fun together as she was growing up. Today she is 18 years old. I was 62 years old and Pam was 40 when Hannah was born.

The Trials and Triumphs

I worked in the record room about one year, a dispatcher's position came open and I applied, got the job and started on the 4pm to 12m shift. It was quite a busy job; I took calls, send cruisers to calls and did this for about 2 years. The 8am to 4pm Dispatcher quit and I got moved to the 12m to 8am shift. I always liked the midnight shift, and was pleased to get it. One night an alarm was set off at the old Alibi Restaurant on the North side of the Square. I sent a cruiser and Sgt Edwards went too. When they got to the scene they could not find any point of entry, then I had remembered that many years before when I had almost fell into the 12 foot drop behind that resturant. I told the Sgt and he sent his men to the West side of the Midland Theater, when they climbed up the fire escape to the adjoining roof that would lead them to the drop off behind the Alibi. They did and when they got to the drop off, the two suspects were there. They couldn't get out as the door to the alley was locked. They had went on the roofs and dropped down to the rear of the Alibi and broke in the rear door and got in, setting off the alarm. They got scared and ran out but couldn't get back up on the roof. We called the owner who came down and unlocked the door and the 2 suspects were arrested for breaking and entering. This was just one of the many stories I have from that job.

I worked as a dispatcher for 15 more years on that shift. I wanted to go to a daylight shift, a records clerk position was open and I applied and got the job. Jim Dean became Safety Director and I came up with the ideas that there should be a Civilian Supervisor over all the civilians working in the department. I talked to Chief Paul Green, who became Chief when Bob Post retired. He thought it was a good idea. I got his permission to talk to Jim Dean, and I told him about my idea. He liked it and told me to write it up and I had it put in there that the supervisor should work directly under the Chief, because I knew that problems would arise if I was under a Captain. I presented it to Jim and he was going to present it to Council, they approved it because it would free a Captain up to do another job. But the ordinance read the supervisor would be under the Chief OR Captain. That was to cause problems at a later time, there were 43 applicants for this job, and I got the job.

July 23, 2000, I was appointed Civilian Supervisor of Records and Communications, it was in the newspaper and Chief Green stated he thought a Civilian Supervisor over civilian workers was a good move. It was hard to overlook Fournier who had almost 50 years with the department. I think he will be a great man for the position because of all the experience he had with Records and Communications. With a lot of law enforcement experience in out department, he was my Captain many years ago. I went to work and gave each records clerk a special job to do. I had a large room in the department for records that we could refer too. I had them all filed by date and got a storage room garage for old records, filed in order at the City Street Department. I don't know how many times I had to go there for old records. I had a small room in the department where we kept our records of all the officers; this was under lock and key. The Communications Officers were doing a good job and I kept tabs on them. I became the LEADS coordinator and had to send reports to the state every month. I really liked that position and it kept me very busy.

Chief Paul Green retired and a new Chief was appointed by the name of H. Darrel Pennington. He had been with the Columbus Police Department and was a nice person, but had his own way of doing things. He put me under the Captain and things began to change. We did not see eye to eye and he was interfering with what I was doing. Every supervisor had to make an evaluation of their men, and he called me into his office and showed me mine. I couldn't believe it, it was the poorest evaluation you could get. I told him that I disagreed with it and he had everything on the lowest level he could. I always worked so hard at what I did. He gave it to me and I took it to the Chief and he couldn't believe it either, and told me he was disregarding it. I took it to Jim Dean and showed it to him and he said to forget about it. I could not do that. In all my 51 years, I had always received and excellent evaluation, that's when I started to think of retirement and in January 2002 I told the Chief and Jim Dean I was leaving. The last thing I did before I retired for good, Tom Huff came to me and showed me an old article about a Newark Police Officer that had been shot on duty about 100 years ago. Years before we had honored 2 other officers who were killed in the line of duty, Harry Beasley and Walter Bosscowan, and I even organized the members of the department to march in uniform form the department to the cemetery where they were buried. We invited members of the families to attend and I felt the need to honor Thomas Roach in the same way. I got the Chiefs permission and on May 21, 2001 a large squad of officers in uniform marched to Mount Calvary Cemetery and put a wreath on his grave stone, saluted and played taps. It was a nice ceremony.

January 28, 2002, Jim Dean sent a memorandum to Major Frank Stare.

Re: Employee Recognition.

I wish to make you aware of the service to the city by Police Communications Supervisor, Robert R. Fournier. He began employment with the Police Department on November 10th, 1949 and he served in the US Navy during World War 2. Mr. Fournier returned to the military for one year period during the Korean War to fight for his country. Upon his return to the Police Department, he rose through the ranks becoming Sergeant, Sgt of Detective, Lieut of Detectives, and was Captain for 12 years. He retired in 1980, after 30 years of service. His retirement was short lived, as a commitment to the city brought him back to his work as a civilian Records Clerk in the Police Department in 1981. Mr. Fournier's knowledge, training, and experience were quickly put to use as he functioned as a Public Safety Officer, and Radio Dispatcher. He eventually became the city's first Civilian Supervisor in the Police Department and is currently in charge of the records and radio rooms. Mr. Fournier's dedication to the Police Profession remains evident as he recently arranged for a plaque to be displayed in the lobby of the Police Department and conducted a ceremony at Mt. Calvary Cemetery honoring Thomas Roach Jr, the first Newark Police Officer killed in the line of duty.

Bob Fournier arrives at work at 6am daily, putting in many hours of hard work, even after his 50 year career with the city. Would you please consider an appropriate method to recognize Mr. Fournier's accomplishments as a public servant.

Signed,
James Dean
Director of Public Safety

In March 2002, I put in my retirement papers and told the Chief I was going to retire April 20, 2002. I got a nice write up in the newspaper. On April 19, the Chief said he would like for me to attend a Council Meeting with him and at that meeting my name was called to come forward. The Mayor read James Dean's memorandum and gave me a key to the city. I addressed the Council and thanked them for honoring me this way; it was a joy for me to have served the citizens of Newark. I will miss it and thank you again. The Council and audience stood up and gave me a standing ovation. I was real touched and got a lump in my throat. After it was over everyone came up and shook hands with me.

Now I will tell you about my wife Pam. She is so wonderful, so beautiful, and so caring and loving. She has a smile that makes my heart jump every time. She so loves to our children, grandchildren and great grandchild. We have a wonderful life and it's no wonder why I love her so much. We have raised our children up, and had them in Sunday school and church service every Sunday. Steve is married and presented us with 4 grandchildren, Emily, Ellen, Ethan and Echelle. Stacy is married and she presented us with 5 grand children, Brittney, Olivia, Josie, Elton and Trenton. Sean is married and presented us with a grandson, Cameron. Emily our oldest granddaughter presented us with a great granddaughter Grace. What a great family the Lord has blessed us with. Every year Pam, the 3 children and I would go on Vacations. We went to Myrtle Beach about 4 or 5 times, to Virginia Beach and Pam and I took a cruise to the Bahamas. The next time we went on a cruise we took Stacy and Sean. Steve was in the Army. It was a 4 day cruise and 3 days at Disney World in Orlando, Florida. We sure had good times.

Now what was I going to do. I wanted to get a part time job where I could help people. A lady at church, Sandy Hayes, was a secretary at Catholic Social Services, and said that they hired drivers to take people who cannot drive because of their age, or being too sick, to doctor's offices. We would also take them to clinics, hospitals and Veterans to VA hospitals and clinics all over the state. It sounded like what I wanted to do, so I applied and was accepted in April 2002. And have been doing that to this day in October 18, 2008. When I started driving, I didn't know how to go anywhere, and now I can go anywhere, Cincinnati, Cleveland, Columbus, Pickerington and Dayton. I like the job and I help people.

In closing the story of my life, I want you to know all the statements I made are factual and true. This is my life, I am not on an ego trip or want credit for the things I did. I just wanted to tell it like it was. I am now 81 years old and in good health. I don't know how much time I have left, but I live for each day that the Lord gives me. I don't worry about tomorrow anymore because tomorrow may never come. I do know I will enjoy each day given to me and I want to stay close to my Lord and serve him the best I can and the best I know how.

I love God's Holy Word, and I read the Bible every day. There are four scriptures that I really love and I will end with those. 1. John 14:1-6, 2. Philippians 4:13, 3. 1st John 4:11-13 and last being Thessalonians 4: 16-18, which reads, it is about the Rapture, For the Lord himself shall descend from Heaven with a shout, and with the voice of the arch angel, and with the trump of God and the dead in Christ shall rise first. Then we which are alive and remain shall be caught up together with them in the clouds, to meet the Lord in the air and so shall we ever be with the Lord.

The Lord I coming back for us, it may be real soon. Look at this world, look at this Country; Abortions, Gay Marriage, Drugs and Large Destructive storms, people turning their back on the Lord, the time is near, we need to be ready. Ill close my story with one question, If Jesus should come right now, would you be ready to meet him?

This is the story of my life, the trials I went through, from my birth in 1927 to now, 2008. And the good things that happened to me, most importantly being when I accepted Jesus Christ as my personal savior. How my life changed completely and the best thing is that I want to serve him the best that I can and the best that I know how.

www.ingramcontent.com/pod-product-compliance
Ingram Content Group UK Ltd.
Pitfield, Milton Keynes, MK11 3LW, UK
UKHW041949230426
12048UKWH00008B/217